Voices from the
Outer Banks

Books by Stephen Kirk

First in Flight: The Wright Brothers in North Carolina

Scribblers: Stalking the Authors of Appalachia

VOICES FROM THE
OUTER BANKS

A COLLECTION OF PERSONAL ACCOUNTS

Edited by Stephen Kirk

John F. Blair, Publisher
Winston-Salem, NC

JOHN F. BLAIR,
P U B L I S H E R

1406 Plaza Drive
Winston-Salem, North Carolina 27103
www.blairpub.com

Copyright © 2015 by Stephen Kirk
All rights reserved. No part of this book may be reproduced in any form or by
any electronic or mechanical means, including information storage and retrieval
systems, without permission in writing from the publisher, except by a reviewer,
who may quote brief passages in a review. For information, address John F. Blair,
Publisher, Subsidiary Rights Department, 1406 Plaza Drive, Winston-Salem, North
Carolina 27103.

Design by Sally Johnson
Cover design by Debra Long Hampton
Cover image © Bruce Roberts

Library of Congress Cataloging-in-Publication Data

Voices from the Outer Banks : a collection of personal accounts / edited by

Stephen Kirk.

 pages   cm. — (Real voices, real history series)

 Includes bibliographical references.

 ISBN 978-0-89587-644-7 (alk. paper) — ISBN 978-0-89587-645-4 (ebook) 1.

Outer Banks (N.C.)—History—Anecdotes. 2. Outer Banks

(N.C.)—History—Sources. I. Kirk, Stephen, 1960-

 F262.O96V65 2015

 975.6'1—dc23

2015010306

10 9 8 7 6 5 4 3 2 1

To Patricia and Edwin Kirk

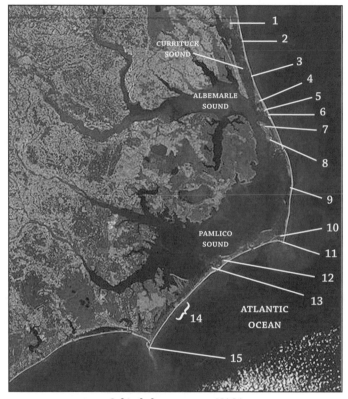

Orbital photo courtesy NASA

1. Knotts Island
2. Corolla
3. Bodie Island
4. Kitty Hawk
5. Kill Devil Hills
6. Nags Head
7. Manteo
8. Roanoke Island
9. Hatteras Island
10. Buxton
11. Cape Hatteras
12. Ocracoke
13. Portsmouth
14. Core Banks
15. Cape Lookout

Contents

Introduction

By one estimate, the Outer Banks has a land area of 391 square miles. Its year-round population is perhaps 40,000. That calculates to about 80 percent of the size and 40 percent of the population of an average North Carolina county.

Considered as an aggregate and viewed in terms of raw numbers, the Outer Banks is a minor landmass, meagerly inhabited.

Moreover, it's a tough place to get to and a tougher place to live. For the majority of North Carolina residents, the South Carolina beaches are closer, more convenient, and more amenity-rich. Parts of the Outer Banks are accessible only by boat. Citizens have to deal with roads that wash out and islands that migrate from underneath the bridges built to reach them. Summer visitors—many from Virginia, the Northeast, and the heartland—should factor in the possibility of an evacuation, as the Outer Banks is the most hurricane-prone region on the East Coast north of Florida.

Why, then, is the area such a draw? The in-season population swells to 300,000, a number that turns over every Saturday with a fresh influx of vacationers arriving for their week at the beach; one estimate places the total at 7 million visitors per year. An Outer Banks seashore park attracts 2.3 million annually. A pier draws 307,000 fishermen.

It must be the sun, sand, and sea.

But all beach communities offer those.

This book suggests that history and tradition make the Outer Banks a destination like no other.

The Outer Banks is the site of the first British settlement in North America and the birthplace of the first English child on American soil.

It's the bloody death site of the most famous of all the pirates, a man still inspiring movies and television series three centuries onward.

It's the site of the first powered airplane flights in human history.

And America's first national seashore.

And the nation's most iconic lighthouse—part of a matched set of four.

It's a place whose names—Kitty Hawk, Kill Devil Hills, Cape Hatteras—are known internationally.

It's "the Graveyard of the Atlantic," in a nod to the rough waters that over the centuries have claimed hundreds of vessels.

It's "Torpedo Junction," site of "the Great American Turkey Shoot," the latter nickname bestowed by German submariners during World War II. Because of their deadly work, a tiny piece of the Outer Banks is British soil today.

In days gone by, the Outer Banks hosted Civil War battles, a freedmen's colony, hunt clubs for the mega-rich, lighthouse families on shore and at sea, and lifesavers who used horses to pull their surfboats to the water and fired lines by cannon to wrecked vessels. To get from place to place, buses, mail and delivery vehicles, and cars drove the beach.

Even now, the Outer Banks is a unique place where ferry transportation remains a way of life and wild horses, perhaps the descendants of ancient shipwrecked animals, roam the sands.

The following chapters present some of the seminal moments in Outer Banks history in the words of people who lived them. Readers will hear the voice of a man who stood aboard a ship and watched Native Americans row from shore to make the first North American contact between the New World and the Old. They'll hear the out-of-state governor who staged an invasion to take Blackbeard's head. And the local postmaster who befriended the Wright brothers and helped set the course of the twentieth century. And the U-boat captain who bumped into one of his victims half a century later. And the former ten-year-old, barefoot beach-bus driver whose size belied his skill. And more than a hundred others.

The term *Outer Banks* is of relatively recent coinage, having come into use perhaps a century ago. Different schools of thought exist as to exactly what it encompasses. One Outer Banks tourist bureau defines it as the string of barrier islands stretching from the Virginia border southward through Ocracoke Island. Another bureau considers it as extending farther, through Cape Lookout; the area would thus include parts of four North Carolina counties—Currituck, Dare, Hyde, and Carteret, from north to south. The late David Stick, definitive historian of the Outer Banks, subscribed to the latter view, as does this book. Which of the small islands approaching the Virginia line ought to be included in the Outer Banks is also a matter of opinion.

This book doesn't claim to present every significant voice from the Outer Banks, or even to treat every worthy subject. Its aim is an overview of the richness of a noteworthy area, expressed in the words of those who discovered its treasures and knew it best. The chapter introductions provide context. Alterations to the text have been made only for readability and limitations of space.

Indeed, little editing was necessary, as it would be difficult to imagine another place that speaks so well for itself—one of such small size packed with such a breadth of history.

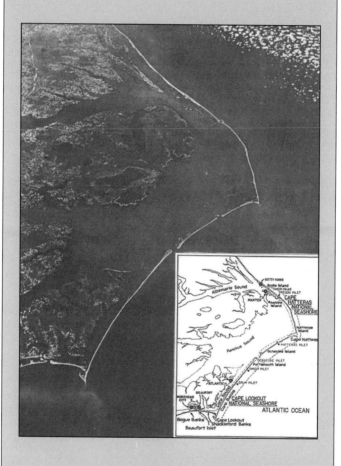

View of the Outer Banks taken by *Apollo 9*

Sir Walter's Legacy

After 425 years, it appeared that America's oldest mystery was solved.

In 2012, a researcher at the First Colony Foundation noticed patches on an old map that he suspected hid something underneath. Scientists at the British Museum subsequently confirmed the presence of a tiny symbol previously unseen. Speculation was that it indicated the site of a fort established by the Lost Colonists after their departure from Roanoke Island.

An expedition sponsored in part by *National Geographic* investigated not to the south on Hatteras Island, where many theories suggest the Lost Colonists migrated, but fifty miles west on the mainland, at the site of an old Native American town, Mettaquem. The archaeologists came armed with ground-penetrating radar and a proton magnetometer, which can detect objects up to thirteen feet underground. They located what were possibly the remains of a cluster of wooden buildings and a palisade.

However, they ultimately admitted the discovery just as likely dated from the eighteenth century as the sixteenth.

Anyone familiar with the various Lost Colony theories wasn't surprised. The 115 members of Sir Walter Raleigh's 1587 expedition were killed in a rampage by Native Americans. Or died at the hands of Spaniards. Or were rescued by local tribes and lived among them, spawning a line of gray-eyed mixed-breed offspring. Or relocated to Georgia or the North Carolina–Tennessee mountains. Or starved. Or were annihilated by disease. Or set sail for England in a homemade boat and perished at sea.

The facts are as follows.

In 1584, Raleigh received a charter from Queen Elizabeth I to establish a colony in North America. He sent an expedition led by Philip Amadas and Arthur Barlowe, which reached Roanoke Island that July and made friendly with the natives. Barlowe returned to England with a pair of Croatan Indians, Manteo and Wanchese.

In 1585, Raleigh dispatched a five-ship expedition under Sir Richard Grenville to the site of his claim. Relations with the Native Americans deteriorated, as the English accused local Indians of stealing a silver cup and retaliated by burning a village. That August, Grenville sailed for England, leaving Ralph Lane and 107 men to establish a colony on Roanoke Island. When Grenville failed to return on time the following April, the colonists sailed to England with Sir Francis Drake, who was returning from a raid in the Caribbean. Grenville reached Roanoke Island shortly afterward and, finding the settlement abandoned, left a small group to maintain Raleigh's claim.

The infamous 1587 expedition was different in makeup and purpose. Led by John White, it had a greater aura of permanence than the previous ventures, as it included seventeen women and nine children among the colonists. And it would linger at Roanoke Island only long enough to retrieve Grenville's men, its destination being Chesapeake Bay, which promised a better harbor.

That plan quickly went awry. All that was left of Grenville's contingent was a lone skeleton. Fort Raleigh on Roanoke Island had been razed. And Simon Ferdinando, the pilot for all the expeditions, refused to transport the colonists onward to the Chesapeake.

It was August by then—too late to plant crops—so John White had little option but to return to England for supplies, leaving the colonists to fend for themselves. Back home, he found England under assault by the Spanish Armada and all vessels needed for the war effort. White was not permitted to sail for North America for nearly three years. Finally arriving at Roanoke Island on August 17, 1590, he and his party discovered only the letters CRO carved into a tree and the legend CROATOAN hacked into another tree near the fort's entrance.

John White discovers the word CROATOAN
carved in the palisade at Fort Raleigh.

Thus was the fate of the Lost Colony, last seen twenty years before Jamestown and thirty-three years before Plymouth Rock. Among the missing was Virginia Dare, the first English child born in the Americas.

The first selection below, from Raleigh's charter, has a strong flavor of English imperial confidence. Raleigh himself never set foot in North America—and, incidentally, never spelled his name *Raleigh* in any of the surviving documents bearing his signature. Once the darling of Queen Elizabeth, he ran afoul of King James during an expedition in search of El Dorado in South America and was beheaded in 1618.

The second and third pieces are from the early, idyllic days of the Roanoke Island venture. In one, Arthur Barlowe recounts the colonists' initial contact with Native Americans; the country was then known as Virginia, in honor of Elizabeth, "the Virgin Queen." The other is Ralph Lane's rave to Richard Hakluyt about the bounty of the new land. An English courtier, author, and compiler, Hakluyt was an important figure in promoting North American colonization, though he never traveled to the New World.

The fourth and fifth pieces are by Thomas Hariot, a young scientist on the 1585 expedition. Hariot learned the Algonquian language from Manteo and Wanchese—the two chiefs who had accompanied the 1584 expedition back to England—and created a phonetic alphabet to transcribe it. While on Roanoke Island, he began writing his *Briefe and True Report*, the first English treatise about the New World. Among his later credits was the first drawing of the moon with the aid of a telescope, an effort in which he preceded Galileo.

The next piece, from Charles K. True's nineteenth-century Raleigh biography, describes Sir Walter in England as he gets his whiskers and his frilly collar doused. The unbidden bath comes after Raleigh has just shown an improbable talent—that of expelling through his ears smoke from Roanoke Island tobacco.

The seventh excerpt reveals how far relations with the natives deteriorated by 1587. It also suggests the dangers the highly vulnerable Lost Colonists—among them Eleanor and Virginia Dare, John White's daughter and granddaughter—were soon to face upon White's departure on his resupply mission. By then, Manteo and Wanchese had gone in opposite directions, the former still a friend, the latter a sworn enemy.

The final excerpt is one man's take on the fate of the Lost Colony. It comes from John Lawson, famed eighteenth-century explorer of the Carolinas and Georgia.

"Charter in Favor of Sir Walter Raleigh, Knight, for the Discovery and Planting of New Lands in America, 25 March 1584"

Elizabeth by the grace of God of England, France and Ireland Queen, defender of the faith, etc. To all people to whom these presents shall come, greeting. Know ye that…we have given and granted…to our trusty and well-beloved servant, Walter Raleigh, Esquire,…free liberty and license from time to time, and at all times forever hereafter, to discover, search, find out, and view such remote, heathen and barbarous lands, countries, and territories, not actually possessed of any Christian prince, nor inhabited by Christian people.…And further that the said Walter Raleigh…shall have, hold, occupy and enjoy…all the soil of all such lands, territories and countries so to be discovered and possessed as aforesaid, and of all such cities, castles, towns, villages, and places in the same…to be had, or used, with full power to dispose thereof…according to the laws of England.…Witness ourselves, at Westminster the five and twentieth day of March, in the sixth and twentieth year of our Reign.[1]

Arthur Barlowe on the first voyage

We remained by the side of this island two whole days before we saw any people of the country: the third day we espied one small boat rowing towards us having in it three persons: this boat came to the island side…and there two of the people remaining, the third came along the shoreside towards us.…He walked up and down upon the point of land next to us: then the Master…and others rowed to the land, whose coming this fellow attended, never making any show of fear or doubt. And after he had spoken of many things not understood by us, we brought him with his own good liking, aboard the ships, and gave him a shirt, a hat & some other things, and made him taste of our wine, and our meat, which he liked very well: and after having viewed both barks, he departed.…As soon as he was two bow shoot into the water, he fell to fishing, and in less than half an hour, he had laden his boat as deep as it could swim, with which he came again to the point of the land, and there he divided his fish into two parts, pointing one part to the ship, and the other to the pinnesse [small boat]: which, after he had as much as he might[,] requited the former benefits received [and] departed out of our sight.

…We fell to trading with them, exchanging some things that we had.…When we showed him [Granganimeo, brother of Chief Wingina] all our packet of merchandise, of all things that he saw, a bright tin dish most pleased him, which he presently took up and clapped it before his breast, and after made a hole in the brim thereof and hung it about his neck[,] making signs that it would defend him against his enemies arrows: for those people maintain a deadly and terrible war, with the people and King adjoining.…

…We brought home also two of the Savages being lustie men, whose names were Wanchese and Manteo.[2]

Ralph Lane to Richard Hakluyt, September 3, 1585

We have discovered the mainland to be the goodliest soil under the cope of heaven, so abounding with sweet trees, that bring such sundry rich and pleasant gummes [gums], grapes of such greatness, yet wild, as France, Spain nor Italy have no greater, so many sort of apothecary drugs, such several kinds of flax, and one kind of silk, the same gathered of a grass, as common there, as grass is here....Besides that, it is the goodliest and most pleasing territory of the world: for the continent is of a huge and unknown greatness, and very well peopled and towned, though savagely, and the climate so wholesome, that we had not one sick since we touched the land here....We find that what commodities soever Spain, France, Italy or the East parts do yield unto us, in wines of all sorts, in oils, in flax, in rosens [rosins], pitch, frankincense, corrans [currants], sugars and such-like, these parts do abound with the growth of them all, but being savages that possess the land, they know no use of the same.[3]

Observations on local fashion, from Thomas Hariot's *Briefe and True Report of the New Found Land of Virginia*

The chief men of the island and town of Roanoke wear the hair of their crowns of their heads cut like a cokes cobe [cock's comb] as the others do. The rest they wear long as women and truss them up in a knot at the nape of their necks. They hang pearls strung upon a thread at their ears and wear bracelets on their arms of pearls, or small beads of copper or of smooth bone called minsal....In token of authority and honor they wear a chain of great pearls or copper beads or smooth bones about their necks and a plate of copper hinged upon a string from the navel unto the mid of their thighs. They cover themselves before and behind as the women do with a deer skin handsomely dressed and fringed. Moreover, they fold their arms together as they walk or as they talk one with another in sign of wisdom. The isle of Roanoke is very pleasant.[4]

A "cheiff Lorde of Roanoac," drawn by John White

Hariot on tobacco

There is an herb which is sowed apart by itself & is called by the inhabitants Uppowoc: In the West Indies it hath diverse names, according to the several places & countries where it grow[s] and is used: The Spaniards generally call it Tobacco. The leaves thereof being dried and brought into powder: they use to take the fume or smoke thereof by sucking it through pipes made of clay into their stomach and head. From whence it purgeth superfluous fleame [phlegm] & other gross humors, openeth all the pores & passage of the body: by which means the use thereof, not only preserveth the body from obstructions; but also if any be, so that they have not been of too long continuance, in short time breaketh them: whereby their bodies are notably preserved in health, & know not many grievous diseases where withal we in England are oftentimes afflicted.

This Uppowoc is of so precious estimation amongst them, that they think their gods are marvelously delighted therewith: Whereupon sometime they make hallowed fires & cast some of the powder therein for a sacrifice: being in a storm upon the waters, to pacify their gods, they cast some up into the air and into the water: so a weir for fish being newly set up, they cast some therein and into the air: also after an escape of danger, they cast some into the air likewise: but all done with strange gestures, stamping, sometime dancing, clapping of hands, holding up of hands, & staring up into the heavens, uttering therewithal and chattering strange words & noises.

We ourselves during the time we were there used to suck it after their manner, as also since our return, & have found many rare and wonderful experiments of the virtues thereof, of which the relation would require a volume by itself: the use of it by so many of late, men & women of great calling as else, and some learned Physicians also, is sufficient witness.[5]

Meanwhile, back on the home front...

One reminiscence of this ill-fated colony is the tobacco plant. When [Ralph] Lane returned with [Sir Francis] Drake he brought specimens of it, and contributed to introduce the custom of using it in England, as it was already more or less prevalent in Spain, Portugal and France. Sir Walter Raleigh was fond of it, and one day he was amusing himself with "drinking" the smoke (that is, taking it into his mouth, and letting it come out of his nose and ears), when his servant came in, and, thinking that his master was on fire, he seized a bucket of water, and dashed it on his head. Elizabeth did not favor its use by her example. One day she made a wager with Raleigh that he could not ascertain the weight of the smoke. He won the bet by weighing first the tobacco used, and then weighing the ashes. The difference was the answer. The queen laughed, and paid the wager, saying "she had heard of those who turned their gold into smoke, but had never before seen the man who could turn smoke into gold."[6]

John White on "the Fourth Voyage Made to Virginia, in the Yere 1587"

The next day we had conference further with them, concerning the people of Secotan, Aquascogoc, and Pomeiok, willing them of Croatoan to certify the people of those towns that if they would accept our friendship, we would willingly receive them again, and that all unfriendly dealings past on both parts, should be utterly forgiven and forgotten. To this the chief men of Croatoan answered, that they would gladly do the best they could, and within seven days, bring the Wiroances and chief governors of those towns with them to our governor at Roanoke, for their answer. We also understood of the men of Croatoan, that our man Master Howe was slain by the remnant of Winginos men dwelling then at Dasamonguepeuk, with whom Wanchese kept company: and also we understood by them of Croatoan, how that the 15 Englishmen left at Roanoke the year before by Sir Richard Grenville, were suddenly set upon by 30 of the men of Secota, Aquascogoc, and Dasamonguepeuk in manner following. They conveyed themselves secretly behind the trees near the houses where our men carelessly lived: and having perceived that of those fifteen they could see but eleven only, two of those savages appeared to the 11 Englishmen calling to them by friendly signs that but two of their chiefest men should come unarmed to speak with those two savages, who seemed also to be unarmed. Wherefore two of the chiefest of our Englishmen went gladly to them: but whilest one of those savages traitorously embraced one of our men, the other with his sword of wood, which he had secretly hidden under his mantel, stroked him on the head and slew him, and presently the other eight and twenty savages showed themselves: the other Englishman perceiving this, fled to his company, whom the savages pursued with their bows and arrows, so fast that the Englishmen were forced to take the house, wherein all their victuals, and weapons were: but the savages forthwith set the same on fire: by means whereof our men were forced to take up such weapons as came first to hand, and without order to run forth among the savages, with whom they skirmished about an hour.

In this skirmish another of our men was shot into the mouth with an arrow, where he died: and also one of the savages was shot into the side by one of our men, with a wild fire arrow, whereof he died presently. The place where they fought was of great advantage to the savages, by means of the thick trees, behind which the savages through their nimbleness, defended themselves, and so offended our men with their arrows, that our men being some of them hurt, retired fighting to the water side, where their boat lay, with which they fled towards Hatorask....

The eight[h] of August, the governor...thought to defer the revenge thereof no longer. Wherefore the same night about midnight, he passed over the water, accompanied with Captain Stafford, and 24 men, whereof Manteo was one, whom we took with us to be our guide to the place where those savages dwelt, where he behaved himself toward us as a most faithful Englishman.

The next day, being the 9 of August, in the morning so early that it was yet dark, we landed near the dwelling place of our enemies, and very secretly conveyed ourselves through the woods, to that side, where we had their houses between us and the water: and having espied their fire, and some sitting about it, we presently set on them: the miserable souls herewith amazed, fled into a place of thick reeds, growing fast by, where our men perceiving them, shot one of them through the body with a bullet, and therewith we entered the reeds, among which we hoped to acquit their evil doing towards us, but we were deceived, for those savages were our friends, and were come from Croatoan to gather the corn and fruit of that place, because they understood our enemies were fled...[and] had left all their corn, tobacco, and pompions [pumpkins] standing [which would be] devoured of the birds, and deer, if it had not been gathered in time: but they had like to have paid dearly for it: for it was so dark, that they being naked, and their men and women appareled all so like others, we knew not but that they were all men: and if that one of them...had not had a child at her back, she had been slain instead of a man....Another savage knew Master Stafford, and ran to him, calling him by his name, whereby he was saved. Finding ourselves thus disappointed of our purpose, we gathered all the corn, peas, pompions, and tobacco that we found ripe, leaving the rest unspoiled, and took Menatoan his wife, with the young child, and the other savages with us over the water to Roanoke.

Although the mistaking of these savages somewhat grieved Manteo, yet he inputed their harm to their own folly, saying to them, that if [they] had kept their promise in coming to the governor at the day appointed, they had not known that mischance.

The 13 of August, our Savage Manteo, by the commandment of Sir Walter Raleigh, was christened in Roanoke, and called Lord thereof,...in reward of his faithful services.

The 18 [of August], Eleanor, daughter to the governor, and wife of Ananias Dare, one of the assistants, was delivered of a daughter in Roanoke, and the same was christened there the Sunday following, and because this child was the first Christian born in Virginia, she was named Virginia. By [that] time, our ships had unladen the goods and victuals of the planters; and began to take in wood, and fresh water, and to new caulk and trim them for England: the planters also prepared their letters and tokens to send back to England.[7]

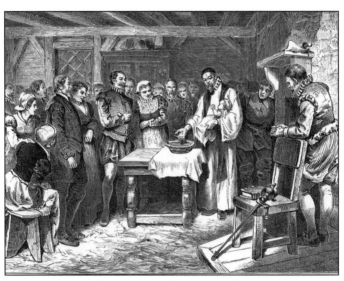

An 1876 lithograph entitled *Baptism of Virginia Dare*

John Lawson speculates about the fate of the Lost Colony in his *History of Carolina, 1714*

The first Discovery and Settlement of this Country was by the Procurement of Sir Walter Raleigh, in Conjunction with some publick-spirited Gentlemen of that Age, under the Protection of Queen Elizabeth; for which Reason it was then named Virginia, being begun on that Part called Ronoak-Island, where the Ruins of a Fort are to be seen at this day, as well as some old English Coins which have been lately found; and a Brass-Gun, a Powder-Horn, and one small Quarter deck-Gun, made of Iron Staves, and hoop'd with the same Metal; which Method of making Guns might very probably be made use of in those Days, for the Convenience of Infant-Colonies.

A farther Confirmation of this we have from the Hatteras Indians, who either then lived on Ronoak-Island, or much frequented it. These tell us, that several of their Ancestors were white People, and could talk in a Book, as we do; the Truth of which is confirm'd by gray Eyes being found frequently amongst these Indians, and no others. They value themselves extremely for their Affinity to the English, and are ready to do them all friendly Offices. It is probable, that this Settlement miscarry'd for want of timely Supplies from England; or thro' the Treachery of the Natives, for we may reasonably suppose that the English were forced to cohabit with them, for Relief and Conversation; and that in process of Time, they conform'd themselves to the Manners of their Indian Relations. And thus we see, how apt Humane Nature is to degenerate.[8]

Blackbeard and Friends

From Kitty Hawk to Ocracoke, visitors won't lack for pirate-themed motels, restaurants, gift shops, and—of course—miniature golf courses. Neither will they have to search high and low for pirate merchandise or strain their ears to hear a pirate legend.

Outer Banks pirate culture is especially impressive considering that it centers on a single man—one who was in the area less than six months, and that three hundred years ago. Blackbeard's stay may have been short, but there is no denying its excitement.

He was born Edward Teach (or Thatch) in Bristol, England, probably around 1680. His literacy and his ease with high officials suggest he may have been from a well-to-do family. He apprenticed for the pirate trade beginning in 1716 in the Bahamas under Captain Benjamin Hornigold, who retired to an honest career about a year later.

Blackbeard arrived on the Outer Banks following the most outrageous exploit of his career, when in May 1718 he led his four vessels in blockading Charleston, South Carolina. The ransom he demanded from the city was mystifyingly small: a chest of medicines. Speculation is that he wanted mercury-based treatments for syphilis—perhaps because he was a sufferer himself. After all, Blackbeard "married" fourteen women, the unions being of dubious legality.

When he sailed that June into Beaufort Inlet just beyond the southern extreme of the Outer Banks, Blackbeard had two purposes. He planned to take a royal pardon and quit the pirate life, yet he also wanted to reserve his loot for himself and his closest comrades. He therefore secreted his valuables on one of his sloops and purposely ran aground his major vessel—the forty-gun *Queen Anne's Revenge*—and a second ship. He then gifted a third vessel to Stede Bonnet, a lesser pirate traveling as his "guest"—his captive, really—and kept only the remaining sloop, the *Adventure*. Then he marooned many of his pirates on a small island and headed north to divide his time between Ocracoke Island and the colonial capital of Bath, on the mainland near the mouth of the Pamlico River.

Colonial citizens had mixed feelings toward "the Brethren of the Coast." Though pirates reserved their worst behavior for the high seas, they were less than model visitors on shore. On the other hand, they provided protection from Spanish and French vessels and brought in quality captured goods at cheap prices. North Carolina governor Charles Eden, also a Bath resident, associated with Blackbeard and even performed his final wedding, to the sixteen-year-old daughter of a local planter.

The Virginia governor, Alexander Spotswood, a man with a personality nearly as outsized as Blackbeard's, undertook to capture or kill the famous pirate. He feared Blackbeard would return to piracy and impact Virginia commerce. He also forecast that North Carolina would become a pirate haven, following a chance meeting in September 1718 between Blackbeard and Captain Charles Vane and the subsequent days-long barbecue and blowout on Ocracoke—the largest-ever buccaneer party on the North American mainland. Spotswood further claimed that North Carolina residents had been writing him that their own governor, Eden, would do nothing to bring Blackbeard to justice.

Spotswood likely exaggerated those complaints. In reality, pursuing Blackbeard allowed him to consolidate power during a period when his legislature was turning against him. And as the governor of a royal colony, he considered North Carolina, a proprietary colony, to be poor, ignorant, lawless, and inferior in every regard. He hoped for a day when the king might purchase North Carolina back from the Lords Proprietors and annex it to Virginia.

That November, Spotswood launched a flagrantly illegal invasion of North Carolina by land and sea. The land force never saw action, arriving near Bath the day after Blackbeard's death. The naval force was comprised of two sloops leased by Spotswood and commanded by Lieutenant Robert Maynard. The vessels caught up with Blackbeard at Ocracoke Inlet at dawn on November 22.

The battle began well for the pirate captain, who lured his pursuers onto a sand bar and raked them with a broadside. The *Adventure* had eight or ten cannons; its opponents had only small arms. But then Maynard outsmarted Blackbeard, a master tactician, with one of the oldest tricks of naval warfare, baiting the pirate into boarding his vessel by hiding most of his men below deck, as if they'd been killed by the broadside.

Blackbeard's men had primitive grenades, but Maynard had superior numbers, especially when his second vessel freed itself and joined the battle. The bloody contest is detailed below. Legend says that Blackbeard's decapitated body swam several times around Maynard's vessel before sinking. The site is known today as Teach's Hole.

The first excerpt is a physical description of Blackbeard. In addition to being an accomplished seaman and a psychological manipulator, he was a sight to behold. The writer, Captain Charles Johnson, is widely believed to have been Daniel Defoe, the British author of *Robinson Crusoe*.

The second piece is the royal pardon under which Blackbeard "retired" to the protection of the Outer Banks and the adjacent sounds. His sincerity is questionable, as he committed what were by his standards minor acts of piracy after taking the pledge, as described in the third excerpt.

The fourth excerpt, also from Captain Johnson, briefly summarizes the buccaneer blowout at Ocracoke headlined by Blackbeard and Charles Vane. Among the all-star attendees were Blackbeard cohort Israel Hands, Robert Deal, and John "Calico Jack" Rackham, soon to be the lover of Anne Bonny and the captain of another lady pirate, Mary Read.

The next piece is the death sentence pronounced in December 1718 on Stede Bonnet, "the Gentleman Pirate," a man *Smithsonian* magazine described as suffering "the worst midlife crisis on record."[1] A wealthy Barbados planter, Bonnet took to piracy, the story goes, to escape a nagging wife. Neither a sailor nor a manager of cutthroats, he was barely competent enough to get himself hanged. Blackbeard played him like a pirate fiddle, taking his ship without a fight and holding him a virtual prisoner on the Outer Banks until tiring of him. Soon after they parted, Bonnet was apprehended by South Carolina authorities, who may have thought they were chasing down Charles Vane.

The sixth excerpt is from one of Governor Spotswood's letters detailing his reasoning for pursuing Blackbeard in North Carolina.

The following piece is a contemporary account of the Battle of Ocracoke Inlet, published in March 1719 in the *Boston News-Letter*, America's first regularly issued newspaper.

The final piece, a sailor's ballad about the battle, is generally credited to the young Benjamin Franklin, who printed it and sold it on the streets of Boston. Franklin's father's ridicule played a part in turning his son to other pursuits. Franklin admitted he would have made a poor poet, though his effort doesn't seem so bad for a thirteen-year-old.

Captain Charles Johnson
describes Blackbeard

It will not be amiss, that we speak of his Beard, since it did not a little contribute towards making his Name so terrible in those Parts.

Plutarch, and other grave Historians have taken Notice, that several great Men amongst the Romans, took their Sir-Names from certain odd Marks in their Countenances; as Cicero, from a Mark or Vetch on his Nose; so our Heroe, Captain Teach, assumed the Cognomen of Black-beard, from that large Quantity of Hair, which, like a frightful Meteor, covered his whole Face, and frightened America more than any Comet that has appeared there [in] a long Time.

This Beard was Black, which he suffered to grow of an extravagant Length; as to Breadth, it came up to his Eyes; he was accustomed to twist it with Ribbons, in small Tails...and turn them about his Ears: In Time of Action, he wore a Sling over his Shoulders, with three brace of Pistols, hanging in Holsters like Bandaliers; and stuck lighted Matches under his Hat, which appearing on each Side of his Face, his Eyes naturally looking fierce and wild, made him altogether such a Figure, that Imagination cannot form an Idea of a Fury, from Hell, to look more frightful.[2]

"Proclamation for Suppressing of Pyrates" under which Blackbeard surrendered, issued by King George I, September 5, 1717

Whereas we have received information, that several Persons, Subjects of Great Britain, have, since the 24th Day of June, in the Year of our Lord, 1715, committed divers Pyracies and Robberies upon the High-Seas,...which hath and may Occasion great Damage to the Merchants of Great Britain, and others trading into those Parts; and tho' we have appointed such a Force as we judge sufficient for suppressing the said Pyrates, yet the more effectually to put an End to the same, we have thought fit, by and with the Advice of our Privy Council, to Issue this our Royal Proclamation; and we do hereby promise, and declare, that in Case any of the said Pyrates, shall on, or before, the 5th of September, in the Year of our Lord 1718, surrender him or themselves, to one of our Principal Secretaries of State in Great Britain or Ireland, or to any Governor or Deputy Governor of any of our Plantations beyond the Seas; every such Pyrate and Pyrates so surrendering him, or themselves, as aforesaid, shall have our gracious Pardon, of, and for such, his or their Pyracy, or Pyracies, by him or them committed, before the fifth of January next ensuing. And we do hereby strictly charge and command all our Admirals, Captains, and other Officers at Sea, and all our Governors and Commanders of any Forts, Castles, or other Places in our Plantations, and all other [of] our Officers Civil and Military, to seize and take such of the Pyrates, who shall refuse or neglect to surrender themselves accordingly.[3]

Captain Charles Johnson on Blackbeard's post-surrender behavior on the Outer Banks

Captain Teach, alias Black-beard, passed three or four Months in the River, sometimes lying at Anchor in the Coves, at other Times sailing from one Inlet to another, trading with such Sloops as he met, for the Plunder he had taken, and would often give them Presents for Stores and Provisions took from them; that is, when he happened to be in a giving Humour; at other Times he made bold with them, and took what he liked, without saying, by your Leave, knowing well, they dared not send him a Bill for the Payment. He often diverted himself with going ashore among the Planters, where he reveled Night and

Day: By these he was well received, but whether out of Love or Fear, I cannot say; sometimes he used them courteously enough, and made them presents of Rum and Sugar, in Recompence of what he took from them; but, as for Liberties (which 'tis said) he and his Companions often took with the Wives and Daughters of the Planters, I cannot take upon me to say, whether he paid them ad Valorem, or no. At other Times he carried it in a lordly Manner towards them, and would lay some of them under Contribution; nay, he often proceeded to bully the Governor, not, that I can discover the least Cause of Quarrel betwixt them, but it seemed only to be done, to shew he dared do it.[4]

Johnson on the pirate party at Ocracoke

Captain [Charles] Vane went into an inlet to the Northward, where he met with Captain Thatch, or Teach, otherwise call'd Black-beard, whom he saluted (when he found who he was) with his great Guns, loaded with Shot, (as is the Custom among Pyrates when they meet) which are fired wide, or up into the Air: Black-beard answered the Salute in the same Manner, and mutual Civilities passed for some Days; when about the Beginning of October [1718], Vane took Leave, and sailed further to the Northward.[5]

Judge Nicholas Trott sentences Stede Bonnet

Major Stede Bonnet, you stand here convicted upon two Indictments of Pyracy; one by the Verdict of the Jury, and the other by your own Confession.

Altho' you were indicted but for two Facts, yet you know that at your Tryal it was fully proved even by an unwilling Witness, that you pyratically took and rifled no less than thirteen Vessels, since you sail'd from North-Carolina....

Not to mention the many Acts of Pyracy you committed before; for which if your Pardon from Man was never so authentick, yet you must expect to answer for them before God.

You know that the Crimes you have commited are evil in themselves, and contrary to the Light and Law of Nature, as well as the Law of God, by which you are commanded that *you shall not steal*, Exod. 20.15. And the Apostle St. Paul expressly affirms, *That Thieves shall not inherit the Kingdom of God*, 1 Cor. 6.10.

But to Theft you have added a greater Sin, which is Murder. How many you may have killed of those that resisted you in the committing [of] your former Pyracies, I know not: But this we all know, That besides the Wounded, you kill'd no less than eighteen Persons out of those that were sent by lawful Authority to suppress you, and put a Stop to those Rapines that you daily acted....

You being a Gentleman that have had the Advantage of a liberal Education, and being generally esteemed a Man of Letters, I believe it will be needless for me to explain to you the Nature of Repentance and Faith in Christ, they being so fully and so often mentioned in the Scriptures, that you cannot but know them....Considering the Course of your Life and Actions, I have just Reason to fear, that the Principles of Religion that had been instilled into you by your Education, have been at least corrupted, if not entirely defaced by the Scepticism and Infidelity of this wicked Age; and that what Time you allowed for Study, was rather applied to the Polite Literature, and the vain Philosophy of the Times, than a serious Search after the Law and Will of God, as revealed unto us in the Holy Scriptures....

And therefore having now discharged my Duty to you as a Christian, by giving you the best Counsel I can, with respect to the Salvation of your Soul, I must now do my Office as a Judge.

The Sentence that the Law hath appointed to pass upon you for your Offences, and which this Court doth therefore award, is,

That you, the said Stede Bonnet, shall go from hence to the Place from whence you came, and from thence to the Place of Execution, where you shall be hanged by the Neck till you are dead.

And the God of infinite Mercy be merciful to your Soul.[6]

The Hanging of Stede Bonnet in Charleston, 10 December 1718, an engraving published in the Dutch version of Charles Johnson's *General History of the Pyrates* (1724)

Governor Alexander Spotswood explains his pursuit of Blackbeard

Having…received complaints from divers of the trading people of that Province [North Carolina] of the insolence of that gang of pyrates, and the weakness of that Government to restrain them, I judged it high time to destroy that crew of villains, and not to suffer them to gather strength in the neighborhood of so valuable a trade as that of this Colony [Virginia]. Having gained sufficient intelligence of the strength of Tache's

[Blackbeard's] crew, and sent for pylots from Carolina, I communicated to the Captains of H.M. [His Majesty's] ships of war on this station the project I had formed to extirpate this nest of pyrates. It was found impracticable for the men of war to go into shallow and difficult channels of that country, and the Captains were unwilling to be at the charge of hyring sloops which they had no order to do, and must therefore have paid out of their own pockets, but as they readily consented to furnish men, I undertook the other part of supplying at my own charge sloops and pilots. Accordingly, I hyred two sloops and put pilotes on board, and the Captains of H.M. ships having put 55 men on board…they came up with Tach at Ocracock Inlett on the 22nd of last month, he was on board a sloop which carried 8 guns and very well fitted for fight.[7]

Boston News-Letter account of Blackbeard's death

Governour Spotswood of Virginia fitted out two Sloops, well manned with Fifty pickt Men of His Majesty's Men of War lying there, and small Arms, but not great Guns, under the Command of Lieutenant Robert Maynard of His Majesty's Ship *Pearl* in pursuit of that Notorious and Arch Pirate Capt. Teach, who made his escape from Virginia, when some of his Men were taken there, which Pirate Lieutenant Maynard came up with at North Carolina, and when they came in hearing of each other, Teach called to Lieutenant Maynard and told him he was for King George, desiring him to hoist out his boat and come aboard. Maynard replyed that he designed to come aboard with his sloop as soon as he could, and Teach understanding his design, told him that if he would let him alone, he would not meddle with him; Maynard answered that it was him he wanted, and that he would have him dead or alive, else it would cost him his life; whereupon Teach called for a Glass of Wine, and swore Damnation to himself if he either took or gave Quarter.

Then Lieutenant Maynard told his Men that now they knew what they had to trust to, and could not escape the Pirates hands if they had a mind, but must either fight and kill, or be killed; Teach begun and fired several great Guns at Maynard's Sloop, which did but little damage, but Maynard rowing nearer Teach's Sloop of Ten Guns, Teach fired some small Guns, loaded with Swan shot, spick Nails and pieces of old Iron, in upon Maynard, which killed six of his Men and wounded ten, upon which Lieutenant Maynard, ordered all the rest of his Men to go down in the Hould: himself, Abraham Demelt of New York, and a third at the Helm stayed above Deck.

Capture of the Pirate, Blackbeard, 1718, by Jean Leon Gerome Ferris, depicts the battle between Blackbeard and Lieutenant Maynard in Ocracoke Inlet.

Teach seeing so few on the Deck, said to his Men, the Rogues were all killed except two or three, and he would go on board and kill them himself, so drawing nearer went on board, took hold of the fore sheet and made fast the Sloops; Maynard and Teach themselves then begun the fight with their Swords, Maynard making a thrust, the point of his Sword went against Teach's Cartridge Box, and bended it to the Hilt, Teach broke the Guard of it, and wounded Maynard's Fingers but did not disable him, whereupon he Jumpt back, threw away his Sword and fired his Pistol, which wounded Teach. Demelt struck in between them with his Sword and cut Teach's Face pretty much; in the Interim both Companies ingaged in Maynard's Sloop, one of Maynard's Men being a Highlander, ingaged Teach with his broad Sword, who gave Teach a cut on the Neck, Teach saying well done Lad, the Highlander reply'd, if it be not well done, I'll do it better, with that he gave him a second stroke, which cut off his Head, laying it flat on his Shoulder[.] Teach's Men being about 20, and three or four Blacks were all killed in the Ingagement, excepting two carried to Virginia: Teach's body was thrown overboard, and his Head put on the top of the Bowsprit.[8]

Blackbeard ballad attributed to Benjamin Franklin

The Downfall of Piracy

…Valiant Maynard as he sailed,
Soon the Pirate did espy,
With his Trumpet he then hailed,
And to him they did reply:
Captain Teach is our Commander,
Maynard said, he is the Man,

Whom I am resolv'd to hang, Sir,
Let him do the best he can.

Teach replyed unto Maynard,
You no Quarter here shall see,
But be hang'd on the Mainyard,
You and all your Company;
Maynard said, I none desire,
Of such Knaves as thee and thine,
None I'll give, Teach then replyed,
My Boys, give me a Glass of Wine.

He took the Glass, and Drank Damnation
Unto Maynard and his Crew;
To himself and Generation,
Then the Glass away he threw;
Brave Maynard was resolv'd to have him,
Tho' he'd Cannons nine or ten;
Teach a broadside quickly gave him,
Killing sixteen valiant Men.
Maynard boarded him, and to it
They fell with Sword and Pistol too;
They had Courage, and did show it,
Killing of the Pirate's Crew.
Teach and Maynard on the Quarter,
Fought it out most manfully,
Maynard's Sword did cut him shorter,
Losing his head, he there did die.

Every Sailor fought while he, Sir,
Power had to wield the Sword,
Not a Coward could you see, Sir,
Fear was driven from aboard;

Wounded Men on both Sides fell, Sir,
'Twas doleful Sight to see,
Nothing could their Courage quell, Sir,
O, they fought courageously.

When the bloody Fight was over,
We're informed by a Letter writ,
Teach's Head was made a Cover,
To the Jack Staff of the Ship:
Thus they sailed to Virginia,
And when they the Story told,
How they kill'd the Pirates many,
They'd Applause from young and old.[9]

A Living from the Sea

The bounty of Outer Banks waters has never been in dispute. "There are plentie of Sturgeons," wrote Thomas Hariot in 1585. "And also in the same months Herrings, some of the ordinary bigness as ours in England, but the most part far greater, of eighteen, twentie inches, and some two foot in length and better."[1]

But such bounty has led to a false assumption. "One of the most common misconceptions about the Outer Banks," noted historian David Stick, "is the belief that commercial fishing has been the primary occupation and source of income in the area since the days of earliest settlement." On the contrary, Stick wrote, "it was primarily a part-time activity, engaged in by the stockmen, pilots, boatmen, and other Banks residents to supply their own needs for food."[2]

The golden age of commercial fishing on the Outer Banks began around the Civil War and lasted the better part of a century. During that period, and barely two weeks into his first Outer Banks visit, Orville Wright remarked on the want-amid-plenty character of local life, as reflected in its fisheries. "The fish are so thick you see dozens of them whenever you look down into the water," he wrote. "The people make what little they have in fishing. They ship tons & tons of fish to…northern cities, yet… about the only way to get fish is to go and catch them yourself. It is just like in the north, where our carpenters never have their houses completed, nor the painters their houses painted; the fisherman never has any fish."[3] Perhaps Kitty Hawk fishermen were too busy pursuing mullet in the ocean or shad in the sound to feed the hungry Wilbur and Orville.

The Outer Banks' isolation retarded the development of the industry before the advent of refrigeration and modern roads, as fishermen were limited to species that were palatable when salted. But once commercial fishing took off, no manner of seafood could peacefully ply the waters or scuttle along the bottom. Various trout and bass species, bluefish, spot, Spanish mackerel, croaker, flounder, carp, eel, porpoise, shark, various turtles, oysters, crabs, clams, scallops, shrimp—all had their turn on the wrong side of a line, net, or other means of capture. For a time, Bankers even dried, baled, and sold seaweed for use as mattress stuffing.

After World War II, such factors as declining yields and employment in tourist-related industries began to drive locals away from what was always a break-even occupation.

In the first excerpt below, Thomas Hariot waxes sixteenth-century eloquent on the Outer Banks' sea bounty and the means of catching it.

In the second, John Brickell, an Irish naturalist who explored North Carolina in the 1720s, describes the "Monsters" of the sea and issues an implicit challenge to Bankers to show more initiative in their pursuit.

The third demonstrates how nineteenth-century residents around Cape Lookout took up that challenge. Orlandah Phillips describes the killing of the right whale known as "Mayflower" in what is remembered as the most epic battle of its kind in state history. The whale's skeleton was donated in 1876 to the North Carolina Museum of Natural Sciences in Raleigh, where it lay in pieces for seventeen years until a taxidermist was hired to assemble it. The task took him three months. The whale hangs in the museum today as its largest and probably longest-running exhibit.

The remaining excerpts concern the fishing scene of more recent times.

In the fourth piece, Sarah Downing recounts Jack Herrington's catch of a record 1,142-pound blue marlin on an Oregon Inlet charter boat in 1974. Those in need of a dose of humility after a big day of Outer Banks fishing need only compare their catches to the lists of local record fish, which are truly amazing. This goes even for Jack Herrington, whose state-record blue marlin has since been surpassed.

In the next excerpt, Northeast resident Susan Van Dongen feels reluctance at the prospect of a vacation at a fishing camp in Cape Lookout National Seashore, only to discover charms she never expected.

In the second-last piece, Beth Finke describes her participation in one of the beyond-number Outer Banks fishing tournaments—in this case a competition for the visually impaired.

The final excerpt places Dewey Hemilright in a setting nearly as perilous as his occupation as a Wanchese commercial fisherman—answering questions from a roomful of eager children.

**Frank Greene etching of a whale on Shackleford Banks
taken at Wade Shore on March 20, 1894**
Courtesy of State Archives of North Carolina

Thomas Hariot on the local bounty

There are also Troutes, Porpoises, Rayes...and very many other sortes of excellent good fish, which we have taken & eaten, whose names I know not but in the countrey language....

The inhabitants take then two manner of wayes, the one is by a kind of wear [weir] made of reedes which in that countrey are very strong. The other way which is more strange, is with poles made sharp at one end, by shooting them into the fish after the manner as Irishmen cast dartes; either as they are rowing in their boates or else as they are wading in the shallowes for the purpose.

There are also in many places plentie of these kindes which follow.

Sea crabbes, such as we have in England.

Oystres, some very great, and some small; some round and some of a long shape: They are found both in salt water and brackish, and those that we had out of salt water are far better than the other as in our own countrey.

Also Muscles, Scalopes, Periwinkles...

Seekanauk [horseshoe crab], a kinde of crustie shell fish which is good meat, about a foot in breadth, having a crustie tayle, many legges like a crab; and her eyes in her back. They are found in shallowes of salt waters; and sometime on the shoare.

There are many Tortoyses both of land and sea kind, their backes & bellies are shelled very thick; their head, feet, and tail, which are in appearance, seem ougly as though they were members of a serpent or venemous: but notwithstanding they are very good meat, as also their egges. Some have been found of a yard in bredth and better.

And thus have I made relation of all sortes of victuall that we fed upon.[4]

John Brickell describes the "Monsters" of the coast

The Whales differ from the Fin-Fish in their Fins. The Fin-Fish having a large Fin on the Back, where the Whale has none, but he has two behind his Eyes, covered with a thick black Skin, finely Marbled….With these two Fins and his Tail he swims and steers himself like a Boat with Oars. The Head of this Monster is somewhat flat, and slopes downwards like the Ridge of a House to the under Lip, which is broader than any part of his Body, and broadest in the middle behind the Bump, for between that and the Fins are his Eyes, which are not much bigger than those of a Bullock, with Eye-lids and Hair like Men's…. He swims as swift as a Bird flies, and makes a track in the Sea like a large Ship under sail. Their Tails do not stand up as the Tails of most other Fishes do, but lie horizontally as those of the Dolphin, and are from three to four Fathom broad.

The middling Whales are about fifty or sixty Feet long, and commonly yield seventy, eighty, or ninety Barrels of Fat or Oil….

These Monsters are very numerous on the Coasts of North-Carolina, and the Bone and Oil would be a great Advantage to the Inhabitants that live on the Sand-Banks along the Ocean, if they were as dexterous and industrious in Fishing for them as they are Northwards; but as I observed before, the People in these parts are not very much given to Industry, but wait upon Providence to throw those dead Monsters on Shoar, which frequently happens to their great advantage and Profit.[5]

Orlandah Phillips recounts the hunt for North Carolina's most famous whale

This particular May Day, they called this one the Mayflower. And it worked itself up in the hook of the Cape [Lookout] where I would say it's only twelve or fifteen foot deep, and it had difficulty maneuvering. And the two pilot boats of course got in shape and put what they called a shackle iron in it. Old Uncle John Lewis…put the shackle iron in and then the whale had to tow the boat….The shackle iron in the whale, if you know what it is, it's a thing about six inches long on the end of a shaft, and when they drive it in the whale, it comes off the shaft and turns crossways and doesn't come out. Well, then they tie it to the boat and wherever the whale goes, it pulls the boat. And then at a time when it was right, they figured the whale's gonna surface, they'd overhaul that line as hard as they can and come up along side of the whale. And at that time they would hit it with…a harpoon….I'd say that the blade was no wider than my two fingers. Long, it must have been a six foot shaft. But they'd pull right up to the side of that whale and just jab it in it, in the vicinity where the lungs were. They called it cutting the lights, and then it would bleed to death. And whenever they'd hit the lungs, it would spout blood, they knew they had that whale to where they could handle him.

Josephus Willis (*pictured here*) and his crew battled and finally landed the Mayflower near Shackleford in 1874.

But this particular May Day whale, named the Mayflower, give 'em so much trouble and fought so hard, the tail knocked the side out of one of the pilot boats...took the whole side right out of it, and the men floating around here in the water. One man got so scared, he went to the other side of the boat that wasn't hurt, was alright, and jumped his full length out of the ocean, getting away from the whale. And the whale had very little danger in it other than hitting it with the tail, and in that case, it tore the boat up. But they had to go get that man first to keep him from drowning, and then go back and pick up the men that was overboard here with the whale. And they still had a hold of the whale....They lanced it and cut the lungs and it bled to death....It was only about twenty five feet of water, and see the whale would be fifty feet....[He] stuck his tail out and flapped it around and bellowed like a bull calf would, like a cow, a bull would. My grandmother said, "We in the light-house felt the vibration of it."They was that close to it and all....

...After they killed the whale and it averaged, say, two miles offshore, and maybe they killed the whale that morning at ten or eleven o'clock, they had to tie a line to it and then two boats with eight men sat there and rowed and pulled that thing ashore. Sometimes it would take 'em more than a half a day to row that thing ashore, making about a mile an hour. Which was another reason that they needed two crews to make an operation. And they had to row and pull that thing ashore, and as the tide would rise, they would keep pulling it closer to shore. You know, right in the surf. Each operation had a little house on the beach....And in the spring they used it to keep their pots and knives and cutting hose in it to render the whale with. And they'd pull that whale ashore, and if they'd get it to shore before night had 'em, maybe three or four hours they'd start to work on it.[6]

Sarah Downing on a state-record blue marlin catch

Some records are meant to be broken while others stand the test of time, and Jack Herrington's world and state record 1142-pound blue marlin caught July 26, 1974 has done both.

Although the world record has been broken, the state record still stands and a mold of the fish, the first Atlantic Blue Marlin taken weighing over 1000 pounds, can be seen in the display case at the Oregon Inlet Fishing Center.

Herrington, of Allison Park, Pennsylvania, had chartered *Jo Boy* out of Oregon Inlet, captained by Harry Baum. "It had been a good dolphin year," Herrington recalled recently, "and I told Harry that we'd love to catch some dolphin."

In the Gulf Stream, they found the long lines of sargassum weed under which the fish swim and the party landed dozens of them. Then they began to troll for marlin and around 10:30 the big fish hit, "and it was a very interesting 2 hours and 45 minutes from that point on," said Herrington....

The marlin made several runs, taking out line before being reeled back in only to then take more line out. Herrington had donned gloves and was thankful that the fighting chair on *Jo Boy* had a foot rest. Mate Richard Baum, Harry's nephew, brought out a brand new harness that Herrington put on to ease the strain of the fight, but the contraption that was supposed to relieve his discomfort in fact created more. It had inadvertently been put on upside down and was burrowing into his side.

Captain Baum kept Herrington's spirits up. "Don't you rest," he told him as he continued to fight the fish. The marlin finally came to the surface on its side, worn out from the long fight. Baum had been on the radio to boats near by, and with the help of one of them, they managed to slide the monster on board around 2 P.M.

On the way back to the fishing center, Herrington began to

Jack Herrington's 1,142-pound blue marlin, caught on July 26, 1974
Courtesy of The Outer Banks History Center, Manteo, N.C.

estimate the weight of his catch. "There was speculation that the fish might weigh more than 1000 pounds. I weighed 160 pounds at that time and I watched that fish, and in my mind started to cut him up into 160 pound portions."

Via radio news began to spread through the fleet and then on shore, and people began to assemble to await the arrival of the big fish. Herrington's wife Phoebe and his three daughters were waiting at the docks. They had heard a large fish had been boated, but didn't know who caught it. The angler could read his wife's lips silently asking, "Who? Who?" to which he silently mouthed "Me! Me!"

...Weighing the fish proved difficult. The scales at Oregon Inlet Fishing Center didn't have enough counter weights, so the fish was loaded into the back of a pickup truck and taken to the Hatteras Marlin Club where it tipped the scales at 1142 pounds, which surpassed the previous record by exactly 300 pounds.

Herrington's world record fell in 1977, when a 1282 pound blue marlin was caught off St. Thomas. Paulo Amorin holds the current world record, a 1402 pounder that was landed in 1992 off Vitoria, Brazil.

When asked how he felt when the record was broken, Herrington responded candidly, "Not badly at all. I always had conversations with myself and I knew records were meant to be broken. I put myself in the same category with the guy who first ran the 4 minute mile or the guy who first climbed that mountain in the Himalayas. I was the first to catch an Atlantic Blue Marlin over 1000 pounds."[7]

"How Romantic Could This Be?" Susan Van Dongen visits an Outer Banks fishing camp

My significant other wanted to show me his favorite place in the world. The most beautiful, romantic spot I could imagine. Paradise. And we would travel there on our first vacation together.

So, I'm thinking maybe Paris? Prague? London?…

"You're going to need waders," John said, "and probably some kind of waterproof pouch for lures, and to keep your bait handy."

Bait? Waders!

"You mean we're going fishing?"

Good-bye, Paris.

Hello, Alger Willis Fishing Camp.

Next thing I knew, we were packing the lantern and nonperishables, shopping for the perfect cooler and a new Penn reel, discussing the merits of live bait. I'm trying to prove my adventurous side, I thought, as well as my devotion.

The Alger Willis Fishing Camp is a collection of unpretentious cabins amid the 30 miles of dunes and sands of the Core Banks, part of the Cape Lookout National Seashore on the Outer Banks of North Carolina....

The camp is across Core Sound from the town of Davis, accessible only by a half-hour ferry ride. Its mystique lies in this isolation. Once you get there—well, that's it. Just the beach, the sky, wildlife and the water, and a handful of fishing fanatics. . . .

Alger Willis—according to Annette Mitchum, his grand-daughter and proprietor of the fishing camp—was a local fellow with a reliable boat who, from the 1940s until his death in the late '80s, gave people a ride across the bay from the mainland.

Earlier in the century the entire beach was owned, the story goes, by wealthy Northerners. Some said it was Rockefellers; some said Roosevelts. At any rate, they were too far away to care. So some of Alger Willis' early passengers staked out their own piece of land and built cabins. Most of these still stand, and—although heavily refurbished—are being used by the fishing camp....

It was a 51-foot boat named the *Captain Alger* that delivered us to the camp, and it was steady as an ark. I enjoyed the ride, keeping an eye out for dolphins, which often frolic in the water alongside of the boats, as if to greet the newcomers.

We docked, and the staff gave us a lift to Cabin No. 2, a barn-like structure with a screened porch that was—except for strips of dunes tethered by the ubiquitous sea oats—literally on the beach. You could get up in the morning, grab your fishing pole, and have sand under your feet before you got the sand out of your eyes....

In Cabin No. 2, the sleeping area was just off the porch, so we could lie in bed and be lulled to sleep by the sound of the surf, just 100 yards away. We also enjoyed the star-gazing from our bunks, looking up through the windows at black velvet skies and luminous stars in all their galactic glory....

Unfortunately for us, Hurricane Marilyn still wreaked havoc, and the current was way too strong for successful fishing. The wind and water pulled our lines this way and that, and even snapped them at one point. But don't let our bad luck dissuade you: We were told that this was a rare occasion at the fishing camp....

So we played horseshoes with giant clamshells and wrote in the sand and built sand castles. We swam and sunbathed and had sand-digger races and dug our feet into the pinkish-tan, wonderfully textured sand....

Everybody connected with the camp was really helpful, and I was reminded of the characters from one of those Pat Conroy novels set on the Carolina coast. Very laid-back.

So were we, after a few days. We slept better, breathed fresh air, ate voraciously, got megadoses of vitamin D in its purest form, and just relaxed.

The Alger Willis Fishing Camp wasn't Paris, but I wasn't disappointed. And for those who treasure unspoiled beaches, starry skies unsullied by light pollution, pelicans and other seabirds, as well as an abundance of fish to challenge any serious surf-fishing enthusiast, maybe Alger Willis really is the most beautiful, romantic place on earth.[8]

Beth Finke on a fishing tournament for the visually impaired

Four hundred to five hundred blind people flinging fishing hooks and bait around? Sounded dangerous to me. But scary and crazy as the Visually Impaired Persons' (V.I.P.) Fishing Tournament sounded, I signed up anyway.

My husband Mike and I had just moved here to the Outer Banks in August along with our son Gus and my Seeing Eye Dog Dora. Little did we know that Nags Head was the site of North Carolina's annual fishing tournament for the blind.

…The tournament began in 1983, and ever since then it has grown both in size and popularity. In other words, a whole bunch of blind folks accept the invitation to come to the Outer Banks and fish. In 1997, I was one of them. I hadn't been fishing since I'd lost my sight 12 years earlier in the summer of 1985. Heck, I had never even fished when I could see!…

When fishing day came, in early October…I started getting nervous.…How would I get onto the boat? Would the boat ride be rough? What if I get sick? What if Dora, my Seeing Eye dog, gets sick? What if the waters get rough? What if the boat capsizes?…

One person noticed my anxiety and reminded me that the boats never go out to the ocean, they stay on the sound for the safety of the participants. Knowing we wouldn't be thrashing around in ocean waves made me feel better.…

…When we finally were told we could get on the boat, my Seeing Eye dog and I practically flew to the steps, we were so eager to get started. "Hold on!" someone yelled to me, "Watch your step!" It was probably the owner of the boat who was doing the yelling, as he seemed very skeptical about what Dora would do in guiding me up and down the steps to the boat. Everyone else there had spent time with Blind people; they all knew how skillfully a guide dog can maneuver even the most unusual paths, like the one that leads you onto a boat. Dora had never been on a boat before, but she guided me beautifully and sat quietly under my bench the entire time I fished.

And that time was l-o-n-g. By the time we were done that afternoon, we'd been on the boat almost 5 hours.…

…[Alan, Beth's fishing partner,] was only 16 years old. He had received an excused absence from school that day to fill his important ham radio position on the boat.

Alan loved to fish, and loved to talk about it. He was born and raised on the Outer Banks.…Before I knew it, Alan had set his ham radio aside and was helping me fish. He was amazingly patient with me, teaching me how to bait my own hooks and then letting me do it on my own....

Alan never once grabbed the pole from me and said, "Here, let me do it." I told him I appreciated his letting me do all this on my own[. H]e answered, "Well, I figured if you're here to learn to fish, you oughtta do it yourself." Ah, out of the mouths of teenagers...

Once I cast my line, I had a hard time feeling whether anything had bitten or not. Over and over again I pulled my line up and over and over again all I could feel on the end was the very bait I had put there myself. Alan watched me struggle with this and finally decided I should forget about feeling for the line to tug near the cranking mechanism. "Just lean over to the end of the pole," Alan instructed, "and feel the line there."

"How?" I asked, leaning over the end of the boat. Amazing to think that a few hours earlier I had been worried about getting seasick. Now I was leaning out of a boat over the open seas, without a care in the world. Well, that's not exactly true, I did have a care. I cared about catching a fish!...

It wasn't long before I did feel a tug. And, of course, Alan was as excited as I was when I pulled that big ol' four ounce pigfish from the water.

"It's a Croaker!" Alan said, "touch it!"

I touched it and heard a distinct "oink!" We both laughed and began a spirited debate about whether my catch was a Pigfish or a Croaker. Whatever the case, I'd never known a fish could make that kind of noise. I'd never known I could catch a fish, either....

Before we knew it, it came time to say goodbye and get off the boat....

...I decided to skip the banquets and stay home, especially seeing as I already had my awards: I'd made a new friend in

Alan, and I'd overcome my fears and learned to fish. It is one thing for me to relearn to do things I used to do when I could see; it's an entirely different thing to learn a new skill, learn to do something I couldn't do even when I had sight.

And the trophy? My 4 ounce Pigfish (or was it a Croaker?), of course.[9]

Kids ask a Wanchese commercial fisherman about his job

Outer Banks native Dewey Hemilright always knew he would not have a 9-to-5 desk job....

"Since 1993, I have always run the same boat, the *Tar Baby*," Hemilright explains. "I bought it about 10 years ago and people always say, 'Good for you, you bought your own boat.' And I say, 'Yeah, but I had more money when I didn't own it!'"

Hemilright fishes up to 100 miles offshore in the Atlantic Ocean from Wilmington, N.C., to Ocean City, Md. His target species include yellowfin tuna, swordfish, mahimahi or dolphin-fish, blueline tilefish, croaker, bluefish, seatrout, grey trout, spiny dogfish, smooth dogfish, bluefin tuna and menhaden....

"I am involved in going to schools in North Carolina, on the coast, and telling students about the day in the life of a fisher-man," explains Hemilright....

Based on his work with youths, *Coastwatch* asked Hemilright to field questions from six curious children....

"How do you make sure to not harm other fish and animals?" asks Kali Morton, an 11-year-old aspiring marine biologist.

"There are different types of gear we use but if it's regulatory discard—a species I can't have or sell—we release them....

Seven-year-old Drew Dube is curious about how many fish Hemilright can catch in a net. Hemilright explains that it is dependent on the species he is targeting. "It could be anywhere from zero to a whole bunch."

Both Kali and Drew want to know the type of bait Hemilright uses. He lists squid, menhaden, Atlantic mackerel, bluefish, artificial squid and spoons as things he uses to catch fish.

Ty Dube, Drew's 4-year-old brother, is more specific. "Do you ever fish with pineapple? Because I caught a catfish once with pineapple."

Hemilright cites a different tropical fruit experience. "I have never fished with pineapple before, but the Chiquita banana cargo ship has come by me when I have been out fishing."

Drew and Ty…are interested in the outer appearance of the boat, as well as certain amenities. They ask about the color of the boat and the engine. Hemilright says that the boat is white, with a yellow Caterpillar engine.

Both boys ask Hemilright if he sleeps on board. Hemilright notes that it depends on the species he is fishing. "Sometimes you can stay out one to five days, depending on the time of year."

Practical Ty asks, "Do you have a toilet on your boat?"

Hemilright chuckles. "No, I do not have a toilet. We just use a 5-gallon bucket and we make sure to not use the same bucket to wash our dishes!" he jokes.

Molly Morgan Johnson, a 6-year-old, is curious about Hemilright's favorite place to fish.

"Since the majority of my fishing is done in the Atlantic Ocean, I like the Gulf Stream on a calm, full-moon night," he says. "You get some pretty nights out there when the moon is full."

Jake Johnson, Molly Morgan's twin brother, asks about the biggest fish Hemilright has ever caught. That would be a 1,200-pound tiger shark. "We released him alive. He was probably 12 foot long!" Hemilright recalls.

Molly Morgan wants to know about his encounters with dolphins.

"You see dolphins quite often, the porpoises. When you're

coming up the channel, coming in from fishing, a lot of times when you're going along at 10 miles an hour, they'll be jumping right alongside the boat," Hemilright says....

Hemilright notes that he has mates who work on the boat and fish with him. But sometimes his sailing companions aren't human.

"One time when I went fishing by myself, I was going real slow out on the water and this kitten jumps up on the washboard, walks down the railing and jumps overboard!...I was 30 miles offshore. I stopped, backed up and netted the kitten up," he continues. "I don't know too many cats that can say they went out fishing."

Molly Morgan, an enthusiastic swimmer, asks if Hemilright likes to swim in the ocean.

"I do like to swim in the ocean," he says, although it's not always for fun. "I'll be 50 miles offshore and have to dive overboard and go under the boat and check something."

Drew is interested in the sequence of events that happens when Hemilright catches a fish.

"Once we catch the fish, we bring them aboard the boat. With the swordfish and tunas, we will clean and process them. After we clean a fish, we pack it in ice," he explains.

"Then we come to the dock, unload catch onto the dock, and at the fish house they will sort the fish based on size and quality. They will then package them up, label them and ship them out to the markets in North Carolina and along the coast," the fisherman adds.

"What is your favorite fish to eat?" Jake wants to know.

"That's a hard question," Hemilright admits. "I like everything really. We're fortunate here in North Carolina to have the variety of species that we have. I like black sea bass, softshell crab, swordfish—just too many to list."...

Molly Morgan asks, "Have you ever seen a mermaid?"

Hemilright chuckles as he responds. "No, but once I thought I did. I have seen a full rainbow while out fishing though. I went to both ends of it and didn't find a pot of gold, so I just kept on fishing."[10]

Hurricanes

They've been the scourge of the Outer Banks through recorded history—and no doubt before that, too.

A hurricane threatened Sir Walter Raleigh's fleet in 1586.

His ships encountered high seas in another hurricane the following year.

John White was tasked with searching out the Roanoke Island colony in 1590 when a hurricane forced him to depart.

And so on.

North Carolina ranks behind only Florida, Texas, and Louisiana among the most hurricane-prone states. The state's capes—Cape Hatteras and Cape Lookout on the Outer Banks and Cape Fear farther south—are particular targets. As a discrete region, the Outer Banks trails only Florida in its likelihood of being hit.

The Atlantic hurricane season extends from June through November; major winter storms are categorized as northeasters. For time immemorial, hurricanes were informally named according to the places they devastated, the ships they sank, the holidays they disrupted, or, most commonly, the years they occurred. They were first identified by women's names in 1953 and then by both women's and men's names beginning in 1979; the practice is fitting, as many hurricane veterans maintain that each storm has a distinct personality. The naming cycle repeats every seven years, though the names of particularly destructive hurricanes may be retired.

Hurricanes generally travel over open water at 8 to 15 miles per hour but can reach forward speeds of 25 to 40. Category One hurricanes pack internal winds of 74 to 95 miles per hour; Category Two, 96 to 110; Category Three, 111 to 130; and Category Four, 131 to 155. Category Five hurricanes have winds over 155 miles per hour and storm surges beyond eighteen feet. Storms change strength as they travel. Though it predated the modern classification system, the great San Ciriaco hurricane of 1899 would have registered as a Category Four at its peak in the Caribbean and as a Category Three when it hit Cape Hatteras.

Hurricanes cause damage by their high winds, their storm surges—that is, the water piled up by their winds, which grows higher as the ocean becomes shallower approaching land—the massive rainfall they generate, and the tornados they spawn. On the Outer Banks, they claim lives, wreck property, disrupt tourism and other trade, inevitably close Highway 12, and alter the landscape itself. "A great majority of the houses on the island were badly damaged," Weather Bureau observer S. L. Dosher wrote of Hatteras Island following the San Ciriaco hurricane. "All the bridges and footways over the creeks and small streams were swept away.... The roadways are piled from three to ten feet high with wreckage."[1]

The first excerpt below suggests the state of storm forecasting before the creation of the United States Weather Bureau in 1870. Folk wisdom was the order of the day. Predecessor of today's National Weather Service, the Weather Bureau was the province of the United States Army Signal Corps within the War Department.

The second excerpt is the shipboard account of a passenger off Capes Hatteras and Lookout during the famous Racer's Storm of 1837. First spotted near Jamaica, the Racer's Storm wandered to the Yucatan Peninsula in southeastern Mexico and along the Texas coast before crossing parts of Louisiana, Mississippi, Florida, and Georgia, reaching the Atlantic, and heading north along the Carolinas. The *Charleston* and its plucky passengers encountered the storm just before it spun northeast to its eventual death in the open sea.

The next piece is a message in a bottle that washed ashore in Bermuda after being tossed from a foundering ship off Cape Hatteras in 1842. The incident likely occurred during the first of two hurricanes that July and August. The fates of the *Lexington*, Captain Morgan, and John Rider are uncertain.

The following piece, by late folklorist Charles Harry Whedbee, treats the legend surrounding the naming of Oregon Inlet, formed during an 1846 hurricane. The more accepted version of the story says the inlet was named for a different *Oregon*, a paddle-wheeler that was the first vessel to pass through the inlet after the storm, in calm water. The same hurricane opened the shallower Hatteras Inlet.

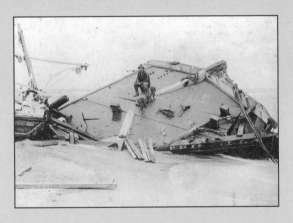

Rasmus Midgett sits on wreckage of the *Priscilla* near Hatteras. He single-handedly saved ten people from this ship during the San Ciriaco hurricane in 1899.
Courtesy of State Archives of North Carolina

The fifth excerpt is the Hatteras weather observer's report to his superior at the Weather Bureau in Washington following the San Ciriaco hurricane. That long-remembered storm sank at least seven ships off North Carolina and was the event that led to the abandonment of Diamond City near the Cape Lookout Lighthouse. Surfman Rasmus Midgett of the Gull Shoal Life-Saving Station won lasting fame for his solo nighttime rescue of ten souls from the wrecked *Priscilla*.

In the next excerpt, Gordon Willis describes a boyhood adventure during the hurricane of 1933, when he partook of a time-honored Outer Banks pastime: salvaging.

The seventh piece collects three Hatteras Island residents' memories of Hurricane Emily, which struck in 1993.

The final excerpt offers a seldom-seen perspective—that of a North Carolina mountain contingent analyzing a hurricane's aftermath. Though Outer Banks residents might take umbrage at the characterization of Hurricane Irene in 2011 as a "small storm" whose "damages were supposed to be petty," the Western Carolina University group's frustration with perpetual rebuilding efforts is shared by many who live away from the coast.

Eighteenth-century weather proverbs, as compiled by the Signal Corps

1. A red sun has water in his eye.
2. When the walls are more than unusually damp, rain is expected.
3. Hark! I hear the asses bray, / We shall have some rain today.
4. The further the sight, the nearer the rain.
5. Clear moon, frost soon.
6. When deer are in gray coat in October, expect a severe winter.

7. Much noise made by rats and mice indicates rain.

8. Anvil-shaped clouds are very likely to be followed by a gale of wind.

9. If rain falls during an east wind, it will continue a full day.

10. A light yellow sky at sunset presages wind. A pale yellow sky at sunset presages rain.[2]

Letter from a *Charleston* passenger during the Racer's Storm, October 1837

The gale…rapidly increased in fury towards night, and the terrific appearance of the billows, with the howling of the wind, convinced me that our situation had become the most serious and dangerous. We were off Cape Hatteras, between 20 and 30 miles from land, in one of the most dangerous parts of the coast of North America….A little before two o'clock in the morning, a sea broke over the stern of the boat like an avalanche; the concussion was so great as to break in the bulk heads, and shatter the glass in some of the windows, far from where it struck. It broke in the sky-lights in the after cabin, and pouring into it in torrents, made a clear sweep over the after deck, as deep as the bulwarks, nearly four feet. The violence of the sea, lifted the deck fore and aft of the wheel house, making an opening about one inch wide the whole length of the boat, through which the water poured into her sponsons every time she shipped a sea, and she rolled like a log in the water. The weather side, moreover, took so much more than the other, that it occasioned her to list over very much, and deranged the workings of the engines. Had these failed, all hope would have been at an end. The Captain behaved with remarkable coolness and decision. He had been on the upper deck, at the helm, all the day and night, exposed to the fury of the winds and waves without any shelter. When we shipped the sea, at 2 P.M., he ran down into our cabin, said he could not be absent from the helm, and that if we wished to save our lives, we must turn to bailing out water, or he greatly feared the boat would be swamped….

…Buckets were procured, and we commenced as fast as we could, but every sea we shipped brought in vastly more than all of us could bail out, and the water soon became so deep as to run into the top of my boots….It now became necessary to put some stopping on the outside, but the boat was shipping such tremendous seas, that it was a work of great hazard. A man, however, was procured to go, who was lashed to the stanchions by a strong rope, but such was the depth of the water on the deck, from the continual washing of the waves, that he could do but little. The boat rolled and pitched so dreadfully that we could scarcely stand even when holding on, and she had shipped so much water that she leaned on the side toward the sea, exposing her to its full action. I stood bailing and handing water from the time it first broke into the cabin, until eight o'clock in the morning, wet to the skin, and nearly ready to sink with fatigue. As the day dawned, the storm raged more furiously, the billows rose as high as our smoke-pipe, and as they curled and broke, fell on us with amazing power. About 10 o'clock the engineer told us he thought the engine could not hold out much longer, she was so disarranged and injured by the heavy shocks of the sea. We knew that, as far as re-garded outward means, this was our only hope of safety, and this intelligence was appalling. Our Captain was collected and energetic, but the winds and waves laughed at the puny power of man, and defied all his efforts….

…The captain, who had stood at his post near the helm, now came down from the upper deck and told us the fury of the storm was such that he feared he could not save the ves-sel, that her upper works were fast becoming a wreck, and as soon as they went she would fill and sink; therefore, if it met the approbation of the passengers, he would endeavor to run her ashore, in the hope of saving our lives. He…assured us he would lose his life to save ours.…

We all procured ropes and fastened them around our bodies, for the purpose of lashing ourselves to the wreck, and having embraced each other, prepared to take our part in the work, and to meet the awful impending catastrophe.…As we were then 25 or 30 miles from shore, the captain's anxiety was, to put the boat in as soon as possible, before she became unmanageable or began to sink. He steered for Cape Lookout, in North Carolina, though he could not tell certainly where he was, but concluded it must be the nearest land, and that it would be as good a place to be wrecked on as any.…With all the steam we could raise, we could not steer for shore, the wind and current carrying us down along shore, but not in towards it; and this proved our safety.…The wind, current, and steam, just served to carry us, under the guidance of a gracious Providence, we knew not whither, but into stiller water. About 9 o'clock at night the sea began to be more calm, though the fury of the storm was not lessened, by which the captain was induced to believe that we had doubled the cape and were coming under its lee. By incessant exertions we now nearly cleared the hold and cabin of water, and as the boat shortly came into comparatively smooth water, the captain thought he would try to weather the night at anchor, thinking the storm might abate by morning. Some protested against this and insisted upon running on shore at once, but the captain would not, as he thought we should all perish in the dark. He therefore steered in towards it, and after running two hours dropped two anchors which held the boat. On weighing these in the morning, we found that the largest one had broken short off, and our safety during the night had depended on a small, and, as we should have thought, very insufficient one. Thus a succession of merciful providences attended us.[3]

Message in a bottle, recovered in Bermuda, October 27, 1842

Schooner *Lexington*, off Cape Hatteras, July 15, 1842. This morning at half past two o'clock A.M., it commenced blowing a strong North Wester, which increased to such a degree that it was certain my vessel could not stand it. At 5 I tried the pumps and found that she made eleven inches. She being an old vessel, worked in her joints. At half past eleven, I determined to leave her with my crew (three men and myself) in our launch; but before leaving sounded the pumps, and found she had increased the water in her hold three feet. I write this and enclose it in a bottle, so that if we should not be saved and the bottle be found, it may be known what became of the vessel and us. At 1 P.M. got into the boat with provisions and water sufficient for six days, having beforehand offered up our prayers to God to protect and save us.

Wm. H. Morgan, Captain
John Rider, Mate[4]

"Ease her off!" Judge Whedbee on the legend of Oregon Inlet

On the morning of September 3, 1846, Captain [Jonathan] Williams conned his square-rigged sailing vessel, *Oregon*, away from the docks at Hamilton, Bermuda, down the broad waters of Great Sound, and out into the open Atlantic Ocean. The vessel carried a mixed cargo of cotton, tobacco, onions, several barrels of whale oil, and a quantity of highly prized juniper lumber known as "Bermuda cedar." Although New York was his destination, Captain Williams set his course west by south and pointed directly toward Cape Hatteras some 580 miles away in order to pick up the northward push of the Gulf Stream to speed him on his way.

The weather did not suit Captain Williams.…The sky was a clear, bright blue, but the barometer had been dropping steadily, and the waves, once the *Oregon* reached the open sea, were the largest the captain could remember seeing. It seemed to him that an ominous sense of foreboding filled the ship and the members of its crew as though some awful thing were about to happen.…

As the schooner sailed ahead, the weather grew steadily worse. The wind increased to a full gale and clouds of black scud began to appear in ragged festoons driving across the sky. What had been a favorable wind now increased to a dangerous gale, and Captain Williams had to order shortened sail and lifelines rigged across his decks to keep his crew from being swept overboard by the huge waves that occasionally broke over the decks.

And then the rains came.

Beginning as a misty drizzle, the rain increased from day to day without letup until it seemed as though the very floodgates of heaven had been opened to allow an almost solid torrent of water to pour into the hapless ship. It was impossible to see the bow of the vessel from the helmsman's position at the wheel.…

By September 7, Captain Williams was completely lost. He knew his schooner should be somewhere between Bermuda and the dangerous waters of Cape Hatteras, but as to his exact location and the distance to the deadly cape, he could only guess. Dead reckoning was impossible.…

…Brave man though he was, his heart and brain were filled with terror. Taking firm hold on the lifeline rigged across the deck, the skipper dropped to his knees beside the two helmsmen struggling to keep the vessel under some sort of control. He prayed with complete sincerity for guidance and for salvation from a sea gone completely mad under the scourge of the screaming wind.…

At that moment…Captain Williams heard a sound that strikes terror in the hearts of all seamen. He heard the awful roar of surf breaking upon a beach, and even though it came from downwind, the roar became louder and louder until it almost drowned out the scream of the wind.

Springing to his feet, Captain Williams put his face almost against the ear of the nearest helmsman and shouted at the top of his lungs, "Ease her off! Ease her off! There are breakers ahead. We'll have to beach her! It's our only chance!"

Nodding his head grimly, the sailor nudged his fellow-helmsman with an elbow, and together they strained to turn the ship's wheel until the *Oregon* was running, like a wild thing, dead before the wind with the towering seas racing at them from astern.

Oceanographers tell us that there is within each hurricane a phenomenon that they call "the surge." This is a giant monster of a wave that springs from the very heart of the storm and drives everything before it with such force that nothing can stand in its way.…As it so happened, this was also the wave that came upon the *Oregon* from astern as she turned her bow toward the beach and made a run for the lives of her crew.

…The huge surge, sweeping all before it, came upon the *Oregon* and lifted her, like a large surfboard, and flung her on the leading edge of the surge up and completely over the barrier beach, the sand dunes, and the trees, dropping her with a thud on a sand shoal in the waters of the sound. At the same time, the surge cut a tremendous gash into the barrier beach and sluiced out thousands of cubic yards of sand into the water behind the barrier reef, piling millions of gallons of sea water up into the sound. Within an hour, the demon wind had shifted all the way around to the southwest. Back came that great mound of water, back through the gap already cut by the storm, dredging it deeper and deeper, until a genuine inlet was cut that very night. Hatteras Inlet was created that same night by that same awful hurricane and has remained open ever since. The *Oregon* remained stuck on her sandbar inside the new inlet until two days later, when the wind and water had subsided enough for her cargo to be jettisoned. Thus lightened, she floated free.

There are other stories about the naming of Oregon Inlet. One respected historian and researcher has painted a beautiful word-picture of a steamboat named *Oregon* paddlewheeling serenely through the inlet, the first ship to pass through after the inlet had been gouged out and the sea had returned to a glassy calm. Most of the old-timers, however, believe that it was Captain Williams' *Oregon* that was hurled through as the inlet was being born and thus lent her name to the new passageway through the barrier.[5]

The Hatteras weatherman describes the San Ciriaco hurricane

August 21, 1899
Chief of the Weather Bureau,
Washington, D.C.

Sir:

I have the honor to make the following report of the severe hurricane which swept over this section on the 16th, 17th, and 18th instantly.

The wind began blowing a gale from the east on the morning of the 16th, varying in velocity from 35 to 50 miles an hour.…During the early morning of the 17th the wind increased to a hurricane and at about 4 A.M. it was blowing at a rate of 70 miles, at 10 A.M. it had increased to 84 miles and at 1 P.M. it was blowing at a velocity of 93 miles with occasional extreme velocities of 120 miles to 140 per hour. The record of wind from about 1 P.M. was lost, but it is estimated that the wind blew even with greater force from about 3 P.M. to 7 P.M. and it is believed that between these hours the wind reached a regular velocity of at least 100 miles per hour....

This hurricane was, without question, the most severe storm that has ever passed over this section within the memory of any person now living, and there are people here who can remember back for a period of over 75 years....

The scene here on the 17th was wild and terrifying in the extreme. By 8 A.M. on that date the entire island was covered with water blown in from the sound, and by 1 A.M. all the land was covered to a depth of from 3 to ten feet. The tide swept over the island at a fearful rate carrying everything movable before it. There were not more than four houses on the island in which the tide did not rise to a depth from one to four feet, and at least half of the people had to abandon their homes and property to the mercy of the wind and tide and seek the safety of their own lives with those who were fortunate enough to live on higher land.

Language is inadequate to express the conditions which prevailed all day on the 17th. The howling wind, the rushing and roaring tide and the awful sea which swept over the beach and thundered like a thousand pieces of artillery made a picture which was at once appalling and terrible and the like of which Dante's Inferno could scarcely equal.

The frightened people were grouped sometimes 40 or 50 in one house, and at times one house would have to be abandoned and they would all have to wade almost beyond their depth in order to reach another. All day this gale, tide, and sea continued with a fury and persistent energy that knew no abatement, and the strain on the minds of every one was something so frightful and dejecting that it cannot be expressed.

In many houses families were huddled together in the upper portion of the building with the water several feet deep in the lower portion, not knowing what minute the house would either be blown down or swept away by the tide....

Cattle, sheep, hogs and chickens were drowned by the hundreds before the very eyes of the owners, who were powerless to render any assistance on account of the rushing tide. The fright of these poor animals was terrible to see, and their cries of horror when being surrounded by the water were pitiful in the extreme....

There has been no communication with this place by wire or mail since the storm, and it is not known when there will be. It is therefore requested that so much of this report as may be of interest to the public be given to the Associated Press for publication in the newspaper.

Very respectfully,

S. L. Dosher
Observer, Weather Bureau[6]

United States Weather Station on Hatteras Island, circa 1903
Courtesy of State Archives of North Carolina

Gordon Willis on the hurricane of 1933

Hurricane of nineteen thirty-three. It started blowin' up hard on a Friday morning....And evidently the Coast Guard heard that there was a bad storm coming, so they come around to everybody left, still left down to the Cape [Lookout] and told 'em all to come up to the Coast Guard Station; leave the houses and camps and all....So we all went on up to the Coast Guard Station. And as the evening progressed, it started blowin' harder and harder....The wind gage [*sic*] had four cups on it that the wind would catch in and whirl it around. It blew one of the cups off and jammed the needle pointer at the speed of the wind and called the wind at one hundred and eleven miles an hour. And it could have blowed even harder than a hundred and eleven miles an hour. But that was one of the hard gusts that blew that cup off. And that's where it jammed. It stayed right there because the other three had it out of balance so it wouldn't turn anymore....They said it shifted the Coast Guard, the new building, said it shifted that about three inches on its foundation....

Wendell [Newton] was about my age. That next morning, Wendell and I knew it had done a lot of damage, a hard wind like that, but we decided to walk down to the shore. It hadn't quit blowin' hard yet, it had just calmed down some....We rolled our pants up, were gonna walk down around the Bight... to see what we could find in the drift, the high water. Course the tide was just about all over the Cape. In fact, it floated one camp away, a fish camp that was down there, it floated that away. It was gone, never been seen no more. But we walked down around the shoreline there. We had to roll our pants down, the wind was still blowin' so hard that the sand, that wet sand, was blowin', and it would hurt real bad hittin' your naked legs....

And we walked on around the head of the cove there on the

shore, and there was the most decoys, and some of the prettiest. And we picked up enough, we piled 'em up. I don't know that there wasn't two or three hundred of the decoys....

Well, it was the hunter's camps from inside down towards Davis and on to Atlantic, Sea Level, all them places, that had their camps on the Outer Banks down there....

It destroyed the camps, and of course what decoys they had in the camps, the storm had floated them on down here....

Wendell and I divided 'em and I brought my part home. I reckon I had a hundred and fifty or more. I brought 'em over here to the Island and put 'em under the porch. We had a porch around our house then. I put 'em under the edge of the porch and evidently those people that had lost their decoys down there, they must've heard about it, about me havin' some. Every now and then somebody would come and say, "I lost some decoys. Can I look and see if any you found was mine?" I tell 'em "yeah go ahead." Course the first come picked up the prettiest, whether they were his or not.... Said "this many is mine." I'd say, "O.K.," let 'em come pick out what he wanted....

I didn't charge 'em nothing. So, I was finally left with about four or five with the heads beat off, or not finished or something...ones nobody else didn't want.[7]

Hatteras Islanders remember Hurricane Emily

Connie Farrow was living on Lester Farrow Road in Frisco during the summer [1993] of Hurricane Emily. She and her toddler daughter, Tiffany, decided to stay with her brother for the duration of the storm in his two-story house. As they were preparing to leave, a neighbor stopped by and commented, "Shouldn't you get some of these things up higher?"

"I have lived in this area for most of 30 years," Connie said.

"We have never had tide in the houses." She later returned home to 18 inches of standing water and numerous ruined photographs, clothes, toys, and other possessions.

While they were staying with her brother, water began flooding the downstairs of the house, forcing them to climb to the second floor. Tiffany kept running to the doorway to watch the water creep up the stairs. With a child's innocence, she joyfully announced, "I'm going swimming!"

Karla Jarvis of Hatteras Village says she and her family have many memories of Emily, but this one has a lighter note:

"Since our daughter was so young, we decided at the last minute to evacuate for Hurricane Emily. I remember that when we got home afterwards, we parked the car and stood in the yard, surveying the damage. It was so quiet. It was eerie…

"Then we heard it—the unmistakable sounds of our three little hens, clucking away. On the morning we had hurriedly left, my husband had put them in a peeler pot and sat the pot on top of a pile of webbing—the highest spot we could find. We ran to the backyard, and sure enough, there they were, poking their little heads in and out of the sides of the pot!

"We're not sure how they made it through the storm. We had about 18 inches of water inside the house so we figured the water outside had to have been over the top of the pot. We joked that they must have taken turns holding their breath and standing on each others' [sic] heads. We'll never know their story, but they sure were three happy little hens that day when we took them out of the pot and let them run free.…

John Alwine of Buxton has many Emily memories and shares this one:

"One of the most memorable things about Hurricane Emily and its aftermath is how I met Dan Rather.

"The morning after Emily hit, the first item on my agenda was to get outside and see how much damage had been done to the house and surrounding area. My home backs up to Buxton Woods. The area is low and usually wet even during a dry summer. The water had risen from the wooded area up to within a few feet of my shop. This was kind of okay because it provided me with a source of water to use to flush the toilets in the house, since there was no water available otherwise.

"Walking around to the front of the house, I saw a large TV satellite truck parked just to the south. Being nosy, my neighbor, Ann Jennette, and I went that way to see what was going on. Low [*sic*] and behold, Dan Rather stepped out of the van, introduced himself, and began asking questions about damage to our property, etc. He walked with Ann and me back to our homes to see the damage firsthand....

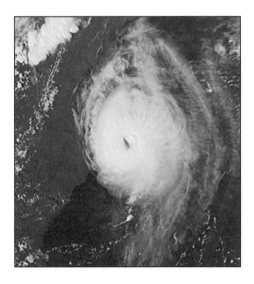

Hurricane Emily heads for the Outer Banks in 1993.
Courtesy of National Oceanic & Atmospheric Administration

John says that a day or two after Emily passed, a neighbor called to ask him to check on the neighbor's waterfront house at the end of Cottage Avenue. "I pulled in under the house as usual, got out, and stepped on a can of beer. I looked around and there was beer everywhere. Every brand you could think of. I walked around the house and found beer in the bushes, laying in the yard, and pooled into piles in low places in the driveway. I checked the house, documented damage, and commenced to pick up beer. Just on my friend's lot, I picked up 175 cans of beer. (Mind you, I only picked up premium brands.) I walked around the neighborhood and found more beer and cans of soft drinks.

"The beer and other items were from a brew-thru type of establishment…that had been hit full force by the hurricane and completely emptied of its contents."[8]

"Foreigners" offer their two cents after Hurricane Irene

Students and faculty from the Program for the Study of Developed Shorelines (PSDS) at Western Carolina University got to see firsthand the damage Hurricane Irene left on North Carolina's Outerbanks [*sic*] the weekend of Aug. 26 [2011].

The program is a research center on campus that takes a worldwide and scientific view of developed shorelines. To analyze the damage of Hurricane Irene, the PSDS took aerial photographs both before and after the storm.

"The comparison of post-storm imagery to pre-storm baseline data allows for quantification of storm-induced changes," said Andy Coburn, Associate Director of the Study of Developed Shorelines.…

Irene had weakened to a tropical storm prior to landfall, and damages were supposed to be petty, yet Coburn was "surprised to see the magnitude and extent of impacts."

Irene flooded and damaged two sections on Highway 21 [*sic*] along the coastline of the Outer Banks and roads were damaged on Pea and Ocracoke Island [*sic*]. There was also significant flooding in the area.

PSDS Director Dr. Rob Young flew over the affected areas following the storm and reported the following details on damages:

1. Hurricane Irene has opened a new inlet just south of the freshwater ponds on Pea Island National Wildlife Refuge on Hatteras Island....There is also a small breach of the island just north of Rodanthe in the Mirlo Beach area. Maintaining Highway 12 in light of even small storms like Hurricane Irene has become an unending challenge for NCDOT. It certainly makes one wonder about the planned replacement of the Bonner Bridge. Even if we can build an immovable bridge, will there be a road left to connect to?

2. The $30+ million beach nourishment project at Nags Head has survived the storm, although there certainly has been some loss of sand along the beach....In our judgment, Hurricane Irene would not have caused significant damage to any properties, with or without the new beach....

Coburn, an expert on coastal management, feels "the coastline does not need to be rebuilt, but if it is, and it probably will be, there is absolutely no reason to put everything back the way it was before since Irene is a preview of what the North Carolina coast can expect in the future."

The PSDS provides information and advice to organizations from state government agencies to nonprofit organizations. PSDS's advice to North Carolina's government includes, "the state needs to be innovative, flexible, and forward-looking rather than preserve the status quo.

"Also, there is no reason to protect or rebuild oceanfront and sound front structures that are damaged and destroyed. The vast majority of these are investment properties and provide very little, if any, benefit to society."

Every member of WCU's community, as North Carolina residents, are part owners of the N.C. coastline under the Public Trust doctrine. Because of this, we are all responsible for the shoreline ecosystems and the species that live there, said Coburn.[9]

Floodwaters from Hurricane Irene cut through portions of Highway 12 on Hatteras Island in August 2011.
Courtesy of the NOAA Hurricane Irene Project

"Feral Pony–Sized Horses"

It's one thing to head to the Outer Banks for a weekend of Nicholas Sparks–inspired romance and healing. It's another to harbor any illusion—as does heroine Adrienne Willis in the screen version of *Nights in Rodanthe*, the New Bern lovemeister's 2002 novel—that a herd of wild horses will materialize to ease the pain. Let's hope those who paid $80 million at the box office and $18 million for the DVD appreciated a Hollywood touch for what it was. Horses haven't wandered Hatteras Island for over eighty years.

Before that, they were everywhere on the Outer Banks. How they came to be there is an ongoing question.

Whether their contemporary descendants should be considered horses or ponies is another.

Whether they've ever been, strictly speaking, wild is a third.

All the theories on the Outer Banks horses agree that they descend from domesticated stock, which technically makes them feral, rather than wild. They measure an average of twelve hands, which places them comfortably within the height range of ponies, most of which stand about fourteen hands. But the term *ponies* properly applies only to specific breeds. And the Outer Banks animals' small size is attributable to sparse feed more than genetics. So it is probably most accurate to say they are "feral pony-sized horses." Outer Banks tour companies can be forgiven for choosing more appealing descriptors.

Horses originated in North America, migrated to Asia and Europe and back again over the millennia, and vanished from our continent for unknown reasons ten thousand years ago. The most popular theory about the Outer Banks horses is that they swam ashore from the wrecks of Spanish treasure galleons from the early to the mid-1500s. Another theory is that Richard Grenville acquired horses from the Spaniards in Española during one of Sir Walter Raleigh's expeditions in the 1580s, only to push them overboard and let them swim for their lives when his fleet ran aground near Ocracoke. Another is that they migrated south after arriving from England with the Tidewater Virginia colonists in the early 1600s.

Regardless of their origin, horses lived free on the Outer Banks for at least three centuries, swimming the inlets from island to island or even washing from place to place during storms. It was a tough existence of eating Spartina grass, digging holes in the sand with their hooves for fresh water, and riding out hurricanes in the sparse forested areas. They were finally removed in the 1930s to preserve vegetation and allow for development.

Three managed herds live on the Outer Banks today. The eighty-plus horses residing north of Corolla are kept from wandering into the village and farther south—as they did before development led to their being hit by cars—by a fence stretching from ocean to sound. Within their range, they roam free to interact with residents and renters of the exclusive, four-wheel-drive-accessed properties on the far northern beaches. On Ocracoke Island, about twenty horses inhabit a 180-acre fenced area next to N.C. 12 south of the Hatteras ferry landing. The facility provides opportunities for viewing and even petting the animals. The most remote herd is on Shackleford Banks in Cape Lookout National Seashore, where over a hundred horses live under conditions approaching a natural state, save for medical monitoring.

The first two excerpts below come courtesy of the Corolla

Wild Horse Fund, whose mission is protecting and managing the northernmost herd on the Banks. The Corolla horses face a complex set of ongoing perils—birth defects from inbreeding, interactions with thoughtless vacationers who may feed or harass them, and opposition from entities that want to cut their numbers, believing them a detriment to the habitat and other species. One excerpt details the Corolla Wild Horse Fund's efforts to secure for the herd the same legal protections enjoyed by the Shackleford Banks horses. The other describes several of the horses available for sponsorship or adoption through the organization.

Wild ponies on Ocracoke Island
Courtesy of The Outer Banks History Center, Manteo, N.C.

The other Corolla piece is a set of instructions for horse seekers who possess four-wheel-drive vehicles but are unfamiliar with the area and the basics of beach driving. Several private vendors operate tours that afford newcomers a better chance of safely seeing the animals.

The first piece on the Ocracoke horses is by Carl Goerch, a native New Yorker who made enough of a mark on his adopted state as a broadcaster, newspaperman, and founder of *The State* (now *Our State*) magazine to wear the moniker of "Mr. North Carolina." Goerch describes the bygone Ocracoke pony pennings, major Fourth of July events until they were discontinued in the late 1950s because of dwindling horse numbers.

The other Ocracoke piece concerns Troop 290, once renowned as America's only mounted Boy Scout troop. The troop's time in the saddle was fleeting, discontinued after about ten years when the Boy Scouts organization insisted all the riders have insurance.

In the first Shackleford Banks excerpt, Carolyn Mason describes the efforts of the nascent Foundation for Shackleford Horses to gain permanent protection for the herd. In 1996, seventy-six Shackleford horses—over 40 percent of the herd—tested positive for equine infectious anemia, a disease that requires strict quarantining. After the infected horses were removed to the mainland, the expense of maintaining them proved unsustainable, and they were euthanized, piled into dumpsters, and buried in a landfill. The negative public reaction led to a grass-roots movement that convinced Congressman Walter B. Jones Jr. to introduce what has come to be called the "Shackleford Banks Wild Horses Protection Act" in the United States House of Representatives. Mason's account tells how major figures in both political parties got behind the effort to safeguard a relative handful of animals on a remote, tiny island.

In the chapter's final piece, novelist BJ Mountford, author of *Sea-born Women* and *Bloodlines of Shackleford Banks*, recounts her experience as a volunteer in the 1999 Shackleford roundup. The last such event was in 2005, after legislation was amended to allow the herd's population to increase to between 110 and 130.

Excerpts from the Corolla Wild Horse Fund's "2015 Fact Sheet"

* There are currently 84 horses. We base our count on an annual aerial helicopter fly-over and comparison to field notes....

* We have requested that the herd size be mandated at the scientifically recommended number of 120–130 with never less than 110....Our request has been denied by US Fish & Wildlife Service and NC Estuarine Research Reserve....

* In January of 2011, and again in January of 2013, United States Congressman Walter B. Jones introduced the Corolla Wild Horses Protection Act. If signed into law, the Act will mandate that the wild horse herd be no smaller than 110 and be managed at a target population of 120–130. It would also allow for introductions of horses from the Shackleford herd to increase genetic diversity. The legislation unanimously passed the U.S. House on Feb. 6, 2012 and was referred to the Senate Environment and Public Works Committee in the Senate on March 21, 2012. The bill was never assigned a hearing.

* On June 3, 2013 the bill was again passed unanimously by the House. On June 4, 2013 it was received by the US Senate. It was never assigned to committee and the year ended with no action taken, despite support from various legislators, the Humane Society of the United States, the ASPCA, Animal Welfare Institute and a host of others.

* The bill was reintroduced into the House on January 5, 2015.

* The wild horses live on 7,544 acres. There is a sound to sea fence at the end of Rt. 12 north of the populated area of Corolla and another sound to sea fence on the North Carolina/VA border.

* We do not intervene in the lives of the horses unless there is a quality of life issue, life and death situation, or something caused by humans.

* We do not supplementally feed them in the winter because they do not need it. If there were starvation issues then we would do a controlled feeding. Once they are fed it changes their physiological and social structure.

* It is against the law to intentionally get within 50 feet of the horses or to feed them. Anything but their native diet may cause painful or even fatal colic. Apples and carrots are not native to their diet.

* The horses' main diet is sea oats, dune panic grass, cord grass, goldenrod, pennywort, acorns, persimmons, and spartina. They also will browse on live oak, bark, and eat the vegetation in the canals.

* The horses drink from ponds, puddles, and the Currituck Sound. The Sound is a fresh water estuarine system. They do not drink sea water unless they are desperately thirsty. It is not a natural defense against parasites nor does it protect them from disease. Just as it can be fatal for humans to consume too much salt water, the same applies to horses.[1]

A sampling of the Corolla horses available for sponsorship and/or adoption

AMADEO—RESCUED STALLION. Amadeo, who had been blind in one eye, lost sight in his other eye after a fight with a rival stallion. Disoriented, he charged into the sea where he nearly died. CWHF partnered with Corolla Ocean Rescue to bring him back to shore.

FELIX—Rescued Colt. Felix's mother was much too young to fully care for him, and it was reported that he may have ingested some stray fishing line on the beach. Small for his age, Felix may reach a mature height of 10 hands. He is known for his playful personality, and he is available for adoption.

NOEL—Rescued Mare. Noel was rescued after becoming stranded in one of the Canals in the Carova area. After rescue, x-rays showed that she had a fractured femur. CWHF brought her in from the wild for care and rehabilitation. Noel is now saddle trained and available for adoption.

VIVO—In the spring of 2014, Vivo was born with contracted tendons. This caused him to walk on his tiptoes, like a ballerina. He was rescued for treatment and he has fully recovered.[2]

Finding the Corolla horses: A tutorial

It is possible to find the wild Spanish mustangs along much of the beach from Corolla to Carova. But most of the nearly 11 miles of beach from the ramp at Corolla to the Virginia line at Carova looks pretty much the same. It is very difficult to know where you are....

You should be mindful of the tide when driving this stretch of beach. Depending on the time of year and the weather, high tide can come very far up on the beach, near the dunes, putting you in deep loose sand with little room to drive. Being able to judge how long it will take to reach Carova or Corolla is extremely useful. Remember, driving along the beach is a lot slower than on the open highway, and you must take that into consideration when judging distance and time. The seemingly short eleven mile drive can often take from 30 minutes to an hour.

Refer to local tide charts to plan your best opportunities for traveling along this beach. At times low tide opens much of this beach to a very wide and hard packed surface, reminiscent of Daytona Beach. At other times, even low tide will give minimal berth, and you must grind your way for miles in soft sand. Also keep in mind that there are no public facilities north of Corolla. No stores, no gas stations, and no public restrooms are to be found....

There is one other hazard you should be aware of that you won't find on most beaches. There used to be an ancient maritime forest where the beach is now. The salt water has preserved many of the stumps from that ancient stand of trees. These are visible at low tide, and can be far enough up on the beach that they could be driven into. These stumps are easily visible in daylight, but may not be so obvious at night. Just be aware that they are present in several places, especially along the southern end of this beach area, and be sure to avoid them....

Though the author had good luck finding horses in the area of Carova, that is not to say the horses cannot be found south of Carova. They range from the Penny's Hill area northward, and are sometimes seen walking up or down the beach along the surf, or grazing on the dunes. With a little planning...and a little luck, you can see these wonderful wild horses for yourself.[3]

Carl Goerch describes the Ocracoke ponies

Anyone who ever has heard of Ocracoke has heard of the wild ponies that roam along the outer banks.

Don't get the wrong idea in connection with the word "pony." These horses are larger than Shetland ponies but they're somewhat smaller than the average-sized horse. Just about the size of polo ponies. As a matter of fact, Ocracoke horses are greatly in demand as polo ponies.

Their origin is uncertain. The story I've been hearing for many years is that a ship was wrecked off Ocracoke Island a hundred or more years ago with several Arabian horses aboard. These animals managed to reach shore safely. They took refuge in the wooded area of the island and gradually increased in number....

They provide their own drinking water in a rather unusual manner. You may not believe this but it's the truth and if you're ever riding or walking about the island you may see it for yourself. Here's what happens:

When the horses get good and thirsty they start digging in the sand with their front hooves. They dig down a couple of feet or so and strike fresh water. Then they proceed to drink their fill....

One of the most widely publicized events on Ocracoke is the annual pony penning. This takes place on the Fourth of July and always attracts a large number of visitors to the island. Late on the night of July 3, five or six men, riding on ponies, leave the village and head for the northern tip of the island. They ride about three hours and then put up in a cabin and spend the night. The next morning they're up at daybreak and, after a bite to eat, mount their horses and proceed to head in a southerly direction.

For the most part the ponies are fairly tractable. With the exception of the young colts they've been through this same experience before and are used to it.

But occasionally some of the horses become balky. They head for the waters of Pamlico Sound and wade out as far as they can—sometimes half a mile or so. One or more of the riders have to follow. Eventually the horses are headed toward the island again and join the others.

The animals approach the village near the Coast Guard station. They thunder along the narrow pavement until they come to the pen which has been built on the shore of Silver Lake near the inn. Amidst much confusion they are herded into the pen and the gate is closed.

The primary purpose of the penning is to brand the colts that have been foaled during the past year. I was somewhat puzzled as to how the colts could be identified as to ownership but the explanation is simple. The young animals never leave their mothers. When a man sees a colt sticking close to the side of one of his mares he knows the little fellow belongs to him.

The youngsters are branded before being turned loose again. Sometimes there are one or more purchasers who desire to buy some of the horses. Otherwise, after having been kept in the pen a couple of hours or so—time enough for everybody to get a good look at them—the ponies are given their freedom and immediately scatter all over the island.

That's how things used to be. In recent years the pony pennings haven't been as big events as they formerly were, due principally to the fact that there aren't as many ponies as there used to be.[4]

The mounted Scouts of Ocracoke, as portrayed in *Boys' Life*

From its population of five hundred, most folks consider that Ocracoke, North Carolina, is a one-horse town. But they haven't heard about Troop 290 and its bank [Banker] ponies.

This tiny fishing village is perched on the Outer Banks of the state at the bottom of Ocracoke Island, a fourteen-mile wedge of sand just south of Cape Hatteras. Here each of the fourteen Scouts in Troop 290 has his own mount—caught, penned, and tamed by the boy himself.

These bank ponies are stunted descendants of horses washed

ashore from a shipwreck off Hatteras in the sixteenth century. A pack of seventy run wild on the island's sand dunes, scavenging for food and digging water holes with their hoofs when they're thirsty. Each summer the animals are rounded up with much ceremony of the Wild East, counted and branded by their owners, then set free to romp the sandbars for another year. But two summers ago, ten of the ponies were bought by Ocracoke boys, and Troop 290 got its start.

Mounted Ocracoke Boy Scout troop
Courtesy of The Outer Banks History Center, Manteo, N.C.

The Scouts tamed these wild horses themselves, going on the advice of Scoutmaster Marvin Howard, who dreamed up the whole idea of a mounted troop.

"These ponies are no easier to break than a western range pony," says Scout Lindsay Howard, who has helped train two of them. "You even have a job lassoing one—if he decides to take off into the ocean. These ponies have grown up next to the sea, and are as much at home in water as on land."

Breaking the ponies is usually a two-man proposition. While one guy holds the horse to calm him down, the other slips on the bridle and then a blanket and saddle. The Scouts often use a T-shirt for a blindfold to help in keeping pony jitters under all possible control.

"Then you get up in the saddle," grins Rudy Auston, "which is either your best or your worst move. The pony is figuring how he's going to throw you, so watch out!"

At first the troop used a dummy, which was made from dungarees with the legs full of sand. But the ponies would buck the dummy off the saddle, and get the annoying habit of kicking it around in the dirt. Considering they'd be the next occupants of the saddle, the Scouts dropped that idea....

Today the Scouts skim across the sand dunes and beach just as skillfully as cowboys span western prairies. And their skill carries over to the care each boy gives his animal.

They feed and stall their ponies in backyards, earning feed costs just as they earned the original fifty-dollar buying price—mowing lawns, working in fish processing plants, heading shrimp, and doing other jobs in town.

They find it costs about $12 a month to keep their steed in feed, not counting the Pepsi Colas—banks ponies are enthusiastic soda drinkers.

At first, acquainting them with civilized feed was a problem. They were used to salt water grass and sea oats. "We actually had to teach them to eat," says Joe Ben Garrish. "They wouldn't touch molasses oats, and we had to stuff the feed down into them."

Scouts are the only islanders who keep banks ponies penned, ready to ride. As a result, they get quite a few calls for unusual service projects. Not long ago when North Carolina Governor Luther Hodges visited Ocracoke, the mounted Scouts formed an honor guard, leading the governor's procession into town from the beach where his helicopter landed....

The troop has nearly all the Scouting-age boys in town. "About the only way to increase the number in the troop," smiles Scoutmaster Howard, "would be to increase the population of Ocracoke."[5]

Carolyn Mason tells of the effort to protect the Shackleford herd

I was running the library at Cherry Point [on the mainland] and one day at the lunch break one of my techs said, "Well, are you going to the meeting today at the Maritime Museum?" I said, "About what?" She said, "They're taking the horses off Shackleford." I said, "Are you serious?" She said, "Yes." I nearly fainted. So I called my boss and I said, "I need to attend a meeting this afternoon and would like to sign annual leave." He said, "Go for it." So I drove down to Beaufort and went to the meeting at the Maritime Museum. And there were some Park people there....

...And they were mentioning this disease called equine infectious anemia, EIA. And they said that they figured at least a third of the horses would have that and they would be euthanized. And I hate that word. Dead is dead and killing is killing. Euthanasia is this smooth sounding word that means you're going to kill the animal. And I've had to put down several dogs and cats that I cried over, but it's still killing and I hate it. I always want them to die before I have to do it.

...At the time the Park was claiming that there were 230 horses over there. Well, I did some quick math and went, "Good God, that's mass murder. That's a lot." And I also was upset over the fact that all my life I'd been told that those horses had always been there. "They were here when our people came," is what the old folks said....

So I just became interested in it and I didn't like the flavor of what was going on. Because everything was downgrading these horses. You know, "They're mutts, they're nags. They're on this tiny little island and we're probably going to kill a third or more of them, and that's OK." And so I started talking to people about it and the Foundation for Shackleford Horses, which is a long name for a small group that works very hard, came into being because of different people that had the same concern....

...I was fifty-two years old when this started. I had never written a legislator, a president, a governor, or even a county official. And that year I wrote all of them and said, "Help. This is not right; these horses need to be here. They are part of this place." And I came in one day and nearly passed out when I touched my answering machine. I came in from work at Cherry Point and this voice on my answering machine said, "Hello, this is Jesse Helms. I got your message and I'm going to look into this about the horses."

...These [horses] are so smart. And you're back in what is survival of the fittest.... See, because horses with bad feet, horses with deformities, horses with, I don't know, intelligence quota lower, they don't make it over there. It's a harsh environment and because of that they are extremely bright horses....

...You get so attached to them; they're so very bright and funny. I swear they have a sense of humor.... They'll do things and when it finally dawns on you what they're doing it just cracks you up. When they look up and look at you with almost a sparkle in their eye, they know they're funny....

...The stars were aligned. We wrote the letters and made phone calls. Beverley [sic] Perdue—the first copy of anything I have is a letter from Beverley Perdue to Congressman Walter Jones. She was a Democratic senator then, he is a Republican Congressman, saying, "Look into this. I can't believe the Park Service [is] upsetting our local friends like they are. See what is happening to these horses." Jesse Helms decided to get in on the act. Congressman Jones, it eventually came to the point that he introduced the Shackleford Banks Wild Horses Protection Act. The entire North Carolina delegation was behind it. Governor Jim Hunt, a Democratic governor, wrote Republican Congressman Walter Jones and said, "Thank you so much. These are part of the state and thank you for introducing this legislation." Governor Hunt also wrote President Bill Clinton and said, you know, these are important to North Carolina. I've got copies of all of those letters, too. And then the vote came and when you think about the gravity of it and how democracy can work, there's this nine-mile long island off the coast of North Carolina with a few wild horses on it, and when it went before the House of Representatives in Washington, DC, that legislation passed by a vote of 416 to 6....Jesse Helms grabbed it and got it through the Senate and it went up to the White House. And who is standing beside Bill Clinton telling him to sign that thing but Erskine Bowles, another North Carolinian. So I said it was like the stars were aligned for that thing to pass and get out there. And once that passed, it was a whole new ball game....What that Bill says is go to the establishing legislation of Cape Lookout National Seashore, go down to paragraph so-and-so and insert, "The Secretary shall allow a herd of free roaming wild horses on Shackleford Banks."[6]

"The 1999 Roundup," by BJ Mountford

January on the Outer Banks of N.C. can be either cold or delightful. A bone-chilling wind was blowing the first day of the 1999 roundup, the sound choppy and leaden. I braced against a rail as the flotilla of park boats, loaded with 50 volunteers, bounced through the frigid water of Back Sound to Shackleford Island, the southernmost barrier island of Cape Lookout National Seashore.

Once disembarked on the westerly end of the island, we walked in groups up the wrack-strewn sound beach to our starting points. I peered hopefully through the scraggly pines and myrtle. Not a horse in sight, not even a little one. Shackleford is home to a band of feral horses whose ancestry can be traced to the Iberian Peninsula—an area that includes Spain, Portugal, Andorra, Gibraltar, and part of France.

At the leader's signal, we formed a thin line and began the sweep across the narrow island, hoping to flush the horses from the thickets to the ocean beach. Not as easy as it sounds. Mud flats, ponds, marshy ground, and extra-thick thickets all had to be checked. I finally spotted my first band of horses— dark, shaggy coated, with long blond manes and tails—but they stayed well ahead, rather to my relief. Wild horses bite and kick, and I wasn't sure how good I'd be at motivating a re- calcitrant horse, even a pony-sized one. We puffed and panted over the sandy hills and finally reached the beach dunes. The brilliant blue ocean with its large breakers crashing on the shore lifted our spirits after the closeness of the thickets. Our job at this juncture was to walk along the ocean-side dunes to discourage the horses from breaking inland, while the ATV crew herded them slowly up the flat beach. We still had six miles to go through soft sand to the fence that crossed the island to the pens.

Once there, we collapsed on some high dunes, where we could observe the procession of horses, some crowded together, many in their bands. One young black stallion wasn't about to be trapped. He danced around the ocean side of the fence, past the yelling volunteers, and bucked over the crashing breakers to escape. Our ranger told us his escape would be short-lived. He and the other strays would be retrieved the following day. Then, all too soon, it was time for us to hike back sound-side to wait our turn for a boat to Harkers Island.

Day two was spent retrieving the strays.

The third day, the tide was too low for the park boat to reach the east dock on Shackelford, so we had to wade in through knee-high water in hip boots that did not fit. There had been a surplus of volunteers for the initial roundup, but the penning and herding of the ponies for testing, identifying, and branding had few volunteers. I was delighted to discover the park needed more hands to work the pens.

Pony penning in Sam Jones's corral on Ocracoke, July 4, 1956
Courtesy of The Outer Banks History Center, Manteo, N.C.

Several years back, the herd had grown to over 200, more than the island could support. Some were starving, others sick with equine infectious anemia (EIA), a disease transmitted by flies. A roundup with testing led to 76 horses being killed. The dispute over this removal resulted in a legislative mandate establishing the Foundation for Shackleford Horses to share management with the park. Horse population would be regulated using birth control and adoption.

This year's tests were being run by two N.C. field vets, the army vet team, their animal handlers, and Dr. Issel from the University of Kentucky. Under the supervision of a horse handler, we'd herd the horses into smaller pens, then into runways. The handler would use his body to hold each horse against the heavy, round rails of the chute, and the vet would crouch below the horse to take blood samples. The vet explained that stallions were all hormones. If they could look down at him, they wouldn't give him any trouble.

Two volunteers remained each night with the horses in case of emergency. This night was my turn. The wind picked up, the heater doing little to warm the tent, but all remained peaceful. The park and vet crews had made sure the horses were watered and fed before they left. The pens had been engineered in irregular shapes to more closely approximate the horses' natural environment—no corners, feeding and water stations placed to minimize problems between the herds.

The park rangers were the first over in the morning and gave us the welcome news that all the horses had tested free of EIA. We helped separate the ponies chosen for adoption and released the rest back to their normal haunts. Shackleford's wild horses were disease-free, the herd reduced to healthy numbers. Birth control could be administered year-round by the use of special darts. The roundup was over; the island belonged to the horses once again.[7]

The Civil War

On July 10, 1861, some slaves were building Fort Hatteras when the cannons of the USS *Harriet Lane* boomed in their direction. Their reaction at taking fire from forces supposed to liberate them is unknown. It was one minor incident in a war of complex motives.

The volleys from the *Harriet Lane*—the first Union shots since Fort Sumter—probably spoke to the strategic importance of the Outer Banks. Early on, the Federals eyed the capture of Oregon, Hatteras, and Ocracoke Inlets, which would give them control of the North Carolina coast and allow the launching of attacks inland. Recognizing this, the Confederates hastened to construct—if not necessarily equip—forts near the inlets and on Roanoke Island.

When a major attack came on August 28, 1861, North Carolina earned the distinction of being the second state—after Virginia—invaded by the Union. A Federal fleet boasting nearly 150 guns and carrying close to 1,000 infantry converged on Hatteras Inlet. Fortunately for the Confederates, Forts Hatteras and Clark stood at the south end of Hatteras Island. Unfortunately, the guns at Fort Hatteras were aimed into Pamlico Sound, leaving the smaller Fort Clark to face the fleet alone. Once the men there used all their ammunition, they abandoned their posts and hightailed it across the sand to Fort Hatteras. The Federals directed their attention to Fort Hatteras the following morning, forcing the outgunned Confederates to surrender before noon. Though not among the war's landmark engagements, the Battle of Hatteras Inlet was the Union's first significant victory.

The incident known to history as "the Chicamacomico Races" occurred in October 1861, during the Federal occupation of Hatteras Island. Given the luxury of 150 years' distance, it is seen as a Keystone Cops–style folly, though the exhausted soldiers no doubt found it less humorous. Upon learning that six hundred men of the Twentieth Indiana were stationed at the isolated village of Chicamacomico (now Rodanthe), the Confederates attacked from the north via Pamlico Sound. The Indianans fled south through the sand to the protection of the Cape Hatteras Lighthouse, a trek of eighteen hours and twenty miles, pursued by Rebels on foot and Confederate ships on the water. The following morning, the Federals counterattacked and the Rebels plodded the twenty miles north back to Chicamacomico, chased by the Indianans on the sand and shelled by a Union ship paralleling their course.

Union encampment at Cape Hatteras Lighthouse

All of this was prelude to the February 1862 Battle of Roanoke Island, in which the largest amphibious force to that point in history—thirteen thousand men aboard nearly seventy vessels—bore down on the lonely landmass between Roanoke and Croatan Sounds. Union general Ambrose Burnside led the assault aboard the USS *Pickett*. Facing him were the seven humble boats of the so-called Mosquito Fleet and fourteen hundred Confederates manning a poorly planned system of forts mostly on the northwest end of the island. When the Federals landed nearly unchallenged at Ashby's Harbor on the west side of the island on the night of February 7, they were within range of only the guns at Fort Bartow, three miles north. The principal action came the next morning at a dirt three-cannon fortification in the swamp at the center of the island, where the Confederates fought bravely but were overwhelmed. Following the victory at Roanoke Island, Burnside moved on New Bern, so as to consolidate control of the entire upper North Carolina coast.

In the first excerpt below, Union admiral David Porter sets the stage for the Battle of Hatteras Inlet and subsequent Outer Banks actions, describing the stakes for both sides, the state of the Federal cause, and the lasting effects of the August 1861 Union victory.

In the second excerpt, Colonel Claiborne Snead of the Third Georgia gives the Southern perspective on the Chicamacomico Races and tells of the after-party in Virginia. Snead idolizes his commander, Colonel Augustus R. Wright, despite Wright's having seized "a small drummer boy that he held in front as a shield" at the height of the action.

The third piece is a paean to Colonel Rush C. Hawkins of the Ninth New York Zouaves. Hawkins was the officer who placed the Twentieth Indiana at Chicamacomico, from which point they raced the Confederates up and down Hatteras Island.

More significantly, he was the glory hound who insisted that his forces captured the dirt fort at the center of the Battle of Roanoke Island, a claim disputed by other Federal units. He and his flamboyant Zouaves wore red fezzes with like-colored tassels. At the time of the writing, Hawkins was temporarily departing Hatteras Island, under arrest and en route to being relieved of command for insubordination. His status was restored shortly thereafter, following a private meeting with President Lincoln.

The fourth piece is a letter from North Carolina governor Henry T. Clark to the Confederate secretary of war asking for reinforcements for Roanoke Island. Dated just six days before the invasion there, it was the latest of dozens of pleas ignored by the higher-ups in Richmond, who realized too late the correctness of Clark's assessment.

The next excerpt is General Burnside's homage to Tom Robinson, the young slave and Roanoke Island native who recommended the Federal landing site at Ashby's Harbor and who provided intelligence on Confederate defenses on the island.

In the following excerpt, culture-shocked journal-keeping corporal David L. Day of the Twenty-Fifth Massachusetts offers a pair of observations on the Outer Banks landscape and Rebel soldiers, the first during the Federal occupation of Hatteras Island and the second shortly after the capture of Roanoke Island.

The final three pieces concern the Roanoke Island freedmen's colony. Following the Union occupation in early 1862, slaves began making their way to the island, where General Burnside granted them freedom and provided them work on construction projects. As the number of former slaves encamped near Union headquarters grew past a thousand by the spring of 1863, Major General John G. Foster, head of the Eighteenth Army Corps, saw the need to formalize a freedmen's colony. He engaged a Massachusetts abolitionist, the Reverend Horace James, as "Superintendent of all the Blacks" in North Carolina. Seeking to establish a self-sufficient colony that would prove a model for others of its kind, James mapped out a village at the north end of the island where the freedmen would build homes on their own land, inaugurated some local industries, and brought in nearly thirty teachers, most from New England. The colony was home to thirty-five hundred people by war's end. The first excerpt is a public letter from James laying out his vision for the colony and soliciting contributions. The second is a letter by missionary Sarah P. Freeman describing one of her young charges. Though most of the colonists migrated from the mainland, some were Roanoke Island natives. The final excerpt suggests some resentment on the part of those natives over being transitioned into new homes and occupations. The formal colony lasted until 1867.

Admiral David Porter on the Battle of Hatteras Inlet

From the beginning the Secessionists had appreciated the necessity of securing possession of the Sounds of North Carolina and defending their approaches against our gunboats. There is in this region a network of channels communicating with the Chowan, Neuse and Roanoke Rivers by which any amount of stores and munitions of war could be sent by blockade runners to supply the South....

The main channel for entering the Sounds was Hatteras Inlet, and here the enemy had thrown up heavy earthworks....

On the 27th of August, 1861, the day after leaving Hampton Roads, the squadron anchored off Hatteras Island, on the extreme southwestern point of which were Forts Hatteras and Clark, separated by a shallow bay, half a mile wide. Of these works Fort Hatteras was the larger, and together they mounted twenty-five guns.

In those days of wooden ships one gun mounted on shore was considered equal to five on shipboard, but even this allowance made the squadron superior to the forts, without considering the heavier guns and better equipments of the frigates.

Part of the troops landed on the island under cover of the guns of the squadron, and at 8:45 on the morning of the 28th, the battle commenced....

...The people in the forts were almost smothered by the fire from the frigates, and their aim made so uncertain, that little damage was done to the ships. Shortly after noon the Confederate flags had disappeared from both forts, and the enemy were evidently abandoning Fort Clark, on which our troops moved up the beach and hoisted the Union flag on that work....

At 7:30, on the morning of the 29th, the ships again opened on Fort Hatteras, and continued the fire with vigor until 11:10, when a white flag was displayed by the enemy....

This was our first naval victory, indeed our first victory of any kind, and should not be forgotten. The Union cause was then in a depressed condition, owing to the reverses it had experienced. The moral effect of this affair was very great, as it gave us a foothold on Southern soil and possession of the Sounds of North Carolina, if we chose to occupy them. It was a death-blow to blockade running in that vicinity, and ultimately proved one of the most important events of the war.[1]

Colonel Claiborne Snead of the Third Georgia on the Chicamacomico Races

On the 1st day of October, 1861, receiving information that a Federal steamer had been seen..., Col. [Augustus R.] Wright at once determined to intercept and capture her; displaying at the very commencement that acuteness of forethought, wisdom in contriving and decision in acting which rendered his subsequent career so brilliant....

By the capture of this steamer, *Fannie*, it was ascertained that the enemy had established a camp at Chicamacomico, on Hatteras Island, forty miles from Fort Hatteras, and near the Southern extremity of Roanoke Island....It was evident the enemy intended the new position as a base of operations against Roanoke Island.

Confederates flee during "the Chicamacomico Races."

Col. Wright seeing a crisis at hand, and appreciating the danger of being isolated and attacked at a disadvantage, promptly determined to move forward and strike the first blow. Passing with his regiment down Pamlico sound, he arrived off Chicamacomico...on the 6th day of October. Nearer to the shore they could not get because of the deep draft of the vessels....Col. Wright, with three companies and two howitzers,…leaping out in the water advanced, wading a portion of the way up to their waists, and opening fire upon the enemy who stood in line of battle upon the beach twelve hundred strong, according to their muster roll.—They retreated hastily and in great disorder in the direction of Fort Hatteras.

The most of our regiment effected a landing in the same way as the three preceding companies, when there commenced a chase which has been properly styled the Chicamacomico races—the enemy running pell-mell for twenty miles, and pursued with a loss to them of eight killed and forty-two captured. At one time Col. Wright, being in advance of the command, overtook the rear guard, who fired upon him, bringing down his horse; but with one hand seizing a small drummer boy that he held in front as a shield, and with pistol in the other hand, he advanced, capturing the Sergeant-Major and four others of his regiment. The daring and skill displayed by Col. Wright throughout the whole affair won the implicit confidence of his men, which he retained during the entire war.

…We were one people, animated by the spirit of liberty and fighting for separate independence, possessing the dash, impetuosity and macurial [*sic*] temperament peculiar to all Southerners of the Caucassian [*sic*] race.…Major General [Benjamin] Huger, the department commander, appreciating the self-sacrificing devotion and arduous labors of [the] men…ordered them back to Portsmouth, which they entered, welcomed by waving handkerchiefs, by martial strains and by roaring cannon. Rome, in her palmiest days, never gave her conquering legions a grander triumph than was awarded the Third Georgia Regiment on that day by the sons and daughters of Virginia.[2]

J. H. E. Whitney describes Colonel Rush C. Hawkins of the Ninth New York Zouaves

Under date of October 31st [1861], Colonel Hawkins is ordered to report to Major-General [John Ellis] Wool, at department headquarters, for trial, which he obeyed on the departure of the first steamer to Fortress Monroe. When the Colonel took his leave the men gathered around him upon the beach and dock, manifesting an unusual degree of love and good-will....

He addressed the men briefly. If he was successful in the trial, he would return to them and take them from Hatteras; if he should fail, he would never return; but in that event commended them to be faithful to a future commander. But he assured them no one would love them or care for them as he had. He seated himself in the boat, and as he was rowed from the shore, waved his fez in reply to the long, loud cheers of the men. The band discoursed an affecting air, and many turned away to conceal the tear that flowed down the cheek, while others eagerly watched the boat until it was a mere speck upon the water.[3]

Governor Henry T. Clark to Confederate secretary of war Judah P. Benjamin, February 1, 1862

Sir:

The various and conflicting rumors about the destination of the Burnside expedition is [*sic*] now settled by its rendezvous at Hatteras....If you will glance at the map you will readily perceive the extent of injury both to North Carolina and the Confederacy by an expedition into the interior from any part of Albemarle or Pamlico Sound. And I regret again to allude to our inability to check so formidable an expedition, whatever route it may select, and I have refrained as long as I could from alluding to re-enforcements. I am aware of the zeal you devote to the immense labors before you, and of the great strain pressing on you from every quarter, and that you would send re-enforcements unasked if you had them to spare.

But I will respectfully tender a suggestion, and be gratified if it coincides with your views; that is, to spare us two or three regiments from the Peninsula, particularly the Fifth North Carolina Volunteers. I make the suggestion on the ground that General [John B.] Magruder has had every facility in men and good, skillful officers for seven months to fortify the Peninsula; that it has been successfully done; that his intrenchments [*sic*], fortifications, and guns have been so successfully and extensively done that they can now be defended with one-half of the men required some months ago; that the place will only allow a defensive warfare, and he is prepared for that, and he can now spare some of his force. A commanding general always asks for more, and never consents to give up a single company. Upon these grounds I refer you to this position, where I hope you can spare at least our own regiment.

I thank you for aid of General [Henry A.] Wise's Legion to the Albemarle country, but I regret to say that Roanoke [Island], not having the benefit of engineers and skillful officers, is not much benefited by the last four months' occupancy by the Confederate Government. General Wise writes to me that it needs everything, whereas it should have been an impregnable barrier to the Yankees and a protection for a great extent of North Carolina and Virginia. There has been culpable negligence or inefficiency at this place....

I tender these suggestions to you most respectfully. Should they fail in enlisting your favor, I shall regret to believe that there are other places besides our coast which claim your protection from overwhelming forces and need more help than we do, for I feel assured of your assistance if it could be spared.[4]

General Ambrose Burnside on runaway slave and Union guide Tom Robinson

How could the troops be landed? Where was the best point for debarkation? These were questions that demanded considerable thought and discussion. They were happily solved by an unexpected reinforcement of intelligence from Roanoke Island itself. A short time before the expedition arrived at the inlet, a negro boy, sixteen or seventeen years of age, came into the camp of our troops at Hatteras. He proved to be a bright, intelligent lad, had escaped from his master, a Mr. Robinson who lived on Roanoke Island, and sought protection from our forces. His name, he said, was "Tom."…Tom knew all about Roanoke and the forts and forces there. There was one strong battery about in the centre of the island. There were two or three others at different points. There were infantry and artillery on the island. There were the "Overland Greys," "Yankee Killers," "Sons of Liberty," "Jackson Avengers," "O.K. Boys"… altogether a pretty formidable array. Did Tom know of a good landing place? "Oh, yes, at Ashby's Harbor, about two miles below Pork Point." Tom knows all about it, has lived not far from the harbor, has been there many a time, and will gladly go there with the troops and show them the way. Up from the harbor is a pretty good road to the place where the rebel battery is. The troops will march up there, drive the enemy out, and take the shore batteries.…

Here was an important auxiliary. Tom's information was particularly valuable. The boy was immediately taken care of, and made to feel that he was no longer a slave.…The very important facts which he imparted were of the greatest service, and most materially aided in accomplishing the success of the movement. He was a quick-witted and bright boy, and he was observed afterwards…conning over a spelling-book of which he had possessed himself, and steadily engaged, at every leisure moment, in learning to read.[5]

The *Pickett* leading the ships of the Burnside expedition
over Hatteras Bar

Corporal David L. Day of the Twenty-Fifth Massachusetts critiques the Banks and the boys in gray

JAN. 19 [1862]…Of all the lonely, God-forsaken looking places I ever saw this Hatteras island takes the premium. It is simply a sand-bar rising a little above the water, and the shoals extend nearly 100 miles out to sea. The water is never still and fair weather is never known; storms and sea gulls are the only productions. Sometimes there is a break in the clouds, when the sun can get a shine through for a few moments, but this very rarely happens. The island…is from one-half to two miles wide, and the only things which make any attempt to grow, are a few shrub pines and fishermen. I don't think there is a bird or any kind of animal, unless it is a dog, on the island, not even a grasshopper, as one would have to prospect the whole island to find a blade of grass, and in the event of his finding one would sing himself to death.…

FEB. 10. The prisoners are a motley looking set, all clothed (I can hardly say uniformed) in a dirty looking homespun gray cloth. I should think every man's suit was cut from a design of his own. Some wore what was probably meant for a frock coat, others wore jackets or roundabouts; some of the coats were long skirted, others short; some tight fitting, others loose; and no two men were dressed alike. Their head covering was in unison with the rest of their rig; of all kinds, from stovepipe hats to coon-skin caps; with everything for blankets, from old bedquilts, cotton bagging, strips of carpet to Buffalo robes....

It is not dress altogether that makes the man or the soldier. I find among these chaps some pretty good fellows. I came across one young man from Richmond; he was smart appearing and very loquacious. In some talk I had with him he said: "This has turned out not as I wished, but not different from what I expected when we saw the force you had....We have met the enemy and we are theirs."[6]

Horace James letter on the establishment of the Roanoke Island freedmen's colony

New York, June 27, 1863

To the Public:

Four days ago, I was ordered by Major-General [John G.] Foster, commanding the 18th army corps, to proceed northward as far as this city and Boston, to collect materials and implements for colonizing the families of colored soldiers upon Roanoke Island....

The exigency now existing in the department of North Carolina, is this: We hold possession of several important places along the coast, the principal of which are Beaufort, Newbern [*sic*], Washington, Plymouth, Roanoke Island, and Hatteras Inlet. At all these points we have troops, and from them our lines extend back some distance into the country. Within these lines dwell large numbers of loyal colored people, and but few whites....It is among these people that Gen. E. A. Wild is now enlisting his African brigade. One regiment is already full, and another is well advanced. As the work goes on, it becomes a question of more and more interest what shall be done with the families of these colored soldiers? How shall we dispose of the aged and infirm, the women and the children, the youth not old enough to enlist in the regiments? In the absence of the able-bodied men to whom they would naturally look for protection and support, it is evident that the government, or benevolent individuals and agencies co-operating with the government, must make temporary provision for them, locate them in places of safety, and teach them, in their ignorance, how to live and support themselves.

The remedy proposed to meet this unique state of things, is to colonize these freed people, not by deportation out of the country, but by giving them facilities for living in it; not by removing them north, where they are not wanted, and could not be happy; nor even by transporting them beyond the limits of their own State; but by giving them land, and implements wherewith to subdue and till it, thus stimulating their exertions by making them proprietors of the soil, and by directing their labor into such channels as promise to be remunerative and self-supporting.

The location decided upon in which to commence this work, in North Carolina, is Roanoke Island. Its insular position favors this design, making it, like the islands around Hilton Head, in South Carolina, comparatively safe against attack, and free from fear of depredation. It is an island ten or twelve miles long, by four or five in breadth, well wooded, having an abundance of good water, a tolerably productive soil, a sufficient amount of cleared land for the commencement of operations, and surrounded by waters abounding in delicious fish.

The time in which to do this work, is the present. It is desirable not to lose a single day....An appeal is hereby made to all the friends of the new social order in the South, and in particular to those who believe that the solution of the negro question is the turning point of the war, for prompt and efficient help in the prosecution of our designs.

The materials required are the same which any colony, designed to be agricultural and mechanical, must need at the start....

Reverend Horace James's Freedmen's School, circa 1865–68

To clothe and educate these people we need quantities of clothing of all descriptions, particularly for women and children, with shoes of large sizes; primers and first reading books, primary arithmetics and geographies, with slates, pencils, and stationery of all sorts....

To fight the country's battles, is our first grand duty. To lay new foundations for a just and prosperous peace throughout the recreant South, is our second. For some time to come the two processes must be carried on together. Let us fight with our right hand, and civilize with our left, till the courage, the enterprise, and the ideas of the North have swept away the barbarism and treason of the South, and made of this country one goodly and free land.

Send contributions in cash, clothing, shoes, instruments, and supplies of every kind needed, to the undersigned at No. 1 Mercer street, New York, (rooms of the National Freedman's Relief Association.)

Horace James,
Supt. of Blacks for the Dept. of N. Carolina[7]

Letter from freedmen's colony missionary Sarah P. Freeman

Roanoke Island, July 7, 1864

One bright little boy was brought to me this morning, with nothing but the remnant of an old flannel shirt to cover him, he had been abandoned by those who brought him from slavery, has neither father or mother, says his name is Jim, and they sold his mammy away from him, when he first heard tell of the Yankees. I asked him what he could do, he says, "I can pull weeds and grass for pigs, right smart, and hold the calves while they milk the cows."... I have set Aunt Sarah at work with him with a tub of water, soap, fine comb, and scissors, and I must set my wits at work to find something to cover him with. He appears to be about six years of age, is black and very bright....

...Our Jim is at length fitted out in a new suit of clothes. But alas the labor it has cost; his little pants consist of twelve pieces, but he is clean and tidily clad, and very happy, so much so, that we do not know how to part with him; he follows me step by step, quietly watching an opportunity to do something for me, and when asked now what he can do proudly answers:

"I can wait upon Mrs. Freeman." Oh, that I had a house large enough to take all the homeless ones. But I know, my Father's house is large enough.[8]

Letter from elderly citizens of the freedmen's colony, December 4, 1866

To the Assistant Commissioner, Bureau Refugees, Freedmen & Abandoned Lands, State of N.C., Raleigh

Sir:

The undersigned freedmen, old citizens of Currituck County, State of North Carolina, born and reared upon Roanoke Island, humbly complaining respectfully sheweth—

That there is a disposition on the part of those whose lands have been restored to them by Maj. Gen. [Oliver O.] Howard to do the undersigned…injustice—in that the aforesaid owners of lands refuse to allow the petitioners to remain upon the land…notwithstanding the fact that the undersigned offer to pay rent or express a desire to purchase lots.

As before stated, born and reared here, the undersigned know only how to make a living by fishing, fowling and "progging"—these being their means of support from their youth to the present day. They are not farmers: this is a sterile section, consequently, but little attention has been paid to agriculture. This being the case, the undersigned, if driven to the necessity of leaving their old home, around which cluster many pleasant recollections—would be able to earn but a poor living, being inexperienced laborers on a farm. The undersigned are sure that you will sympathize with them. They know not what to do in the matter, neither do they know where to go—indeed they here ask whether they shall be made to leave their birth-place, merely to gratify the whims of men who are not well-affected towards the government of the United States.

They therefore ask that you will take such action in this matter as will insure [*sic*] the undersigned justice—protect them in
everything they may do in a lawful manner, or rather, see to it,
that, by paying reasonable rent, they will be permitted to reside
where it is their wish to spend their days, and "when life's fitful
fever's over," lay their bones to mingle with the dust of their
childhood's home.

[Marked by Joseph Tillett and fifteen others][9]

The Lighthouses

Within a short span in the late 1860s, the *Ida Nicholson* went down in a gale off Cape Hatteras, the *J. Parker* washed ashore at Nags Head, and a smaller vessel capsized in Pamlico Sound.

The common irony? All three bore construction materials for the new Cape Hatteras Lighthouse. Perhaps those wrecks and their lost loads of bricks and granite are all the testimony necessary to affirm the need for beacons along the Outer Banks.

In a way, the longevity, beauty, and efficiency of the major Cape Lookout, Cape Hatteras, Bodie Island, and Currituck Beach Lighthouses misrepresent the checkered history of Outer Banks beacons. They are merely the last—and by far the best—representatives of their kind. Preceding them were a number of less successful lights on or near the same sites, along with a haphazardly executed network of beacons stretching east into the Atlantic and west into the channels through the sounds.

Early island-based beacons were short and underpowered. Ship captains sometimes grounded on the shoals looking for them. Lightships were run into by commercial vessels. Prone to breaking loose in storms and drifting or crashing, they were out of commission nearly as often as they were operational.

And then, soon after the Light House Board was established in the 1850s to inaugurate a better system, retreating Confederates destroyed or disabled the very lights that locals and shippers had been pleading for.

Five Outer Banks lighthouses stand today.

The Ocracoke Light Station, completed in 1823 at a height of seventy-five feet, is the nation's second-oldest lighthouse in continuous operation. Its primary purpose was to aid traffic not on the Atlantic but rather through Ocracoke Inlet, south of the island. It is pearl white and emits a constant beacon.

Currituck Beach Lighthouse
U.S. Coast Guard Archive

The Cape Lookout Lighthouse, completed in 1859 at a height of 163 feet, was the first and southernmost of the four major lighthouses and the prototype for the others.

After the Civil War, the Light House Board resolved to address the hazardous stretch from Cape Hatteras northward to Cape Henry, Virginia, at the mouth of Chesapeake Bay. Given priority, the Cape Hatteras Lighthouse was completed in 1870 at 198 feet. Two more lighthouses were then built at forty-mile intervals, at Bodie Island and Currituck Beach. The former was completed in 1872 at 165 feet, the latter in 1875 at 162 feet.

All the new lighthouses were red brick, which created confusion among mariners, who needed to be able to distinguish them both day and night. In 1873, the Light House Board resolved to paint Cape Lookout in black and white checks, Cape

Hatteras in black and white spiral bands, and Bodie Island in black and white horizontal bands; Currituck Beach, still under construction, would be left unpainted. Cape Lookout would flash every fifteen seconds and Cape Hatteras every seven and a half seconds. Bodie Island would flash two and a half seconds on, then the same interval off, then the same interval on, then twenty-two and a half seconds off, for an even two cycles per minute. Currituck Beach would flash five seconds on and fifteen seconds off.

During their years of toting whale oil up the circular stairways and meticulously polishing the lenses, lighthouse keepers were vital figures. But as the lights were automated, keepers' roles diminished. And as commercial vessels and pleasure craft began carrying shipboard navigation systems, the lighthouses themselves grew superfluous. Nonetheless, all five Outer Banks lighthouses today remain as beloved as ever.

The first excerpt below is a selection from the voluminous official instructions given to keepers. The instructions ranged from basic responsibilities to highly technical details pertaining to the upkeep of complicated equipment—and even tips for making one's own whitewash.

In the second excerpt, Orlandah Phillips relates a rather gruesome and unexpected tale of "child's play" from olden days at the Cape Lookout Lighthouse.

Duty aboard lightships was lonely, dangerous, and claustrophobic. Some crewmen likened it to prison. Since the vessels rode at anchor, they were buffeted during storms, when seasickness became rampant. The third excerpt details a rarer but deadlier hazard—that of being torpedoed during wartime.

The next piece is from the period after the lighthouses came under the Coast Guard's purview. William Tate, civic leader and benefactor of the Wright brothers, served as a lighthouse inspector in the late 1930s, based out of the light station at

Coinjock, on the mainland opposite Corolla. He describes one of his duties—a periodic boat trip across the sound to charge the batteries at the then-vacant Currituck Beach Lighthouse. His account suggests how much automation had diminished the duties there.

The final three excerpts concern the Cape Hatteras Lighthouse before, during, and after its heyday as America's most famous beacon.

Bodie Island Lighthouse
U.S. Coast Guard Archive

The Ben Dixon MacNeill piece describes the construction phase. MacNeill notes the lack of pilings supporting the lighthouse. The massive structure was built on a "floating foundation" of submerged but water-resistant pine timbers. Amazingly, the foundation showed no deterioration when examined a century onward. MacNeill also discusses the supposed paint-job mix-up between the Cape Hatteras and Cape Lookout lights, an oft-repeated story that is likely untrue. A noted newspaperman, author, and publicity director for *The Lost Colony*, MacNeill lived out his later years in a small cottage near the Cape Hatteras Lighthouse.

The long piece is from the memoirs of Rany Jennett, whose forbears sold the land for the original 1803 lighthouse at Cape Hatteras. Rany's father, Unaka B. Jennett, was the last principal keeper at Cape Hatteras, serving from 1919 until the lighthouse was transferred to the Coast Guard in 1939. Rany Jennett, born in the keeper's quarters in 1921, came full circle when he returned as a seasonal ranger at the lighthouse in 1984. He married lighthouse volunteer Lynn O'Neill on the property in 1995 and passed away in 2001.

The Outer Banks migrate from the northeast toward the southwest. Erosion became acute near the Cape Hatteras Lighthouse, which stood 1,500 feet from the ocean when constructed in 1870 but just 120 feet away a century later. In 1999, the 129-year-old, 4,830-ton lighthouse was finally lifted, put on rails, and moved 2,900 feet southwest. The relocation has proven such a success that it is easy to forget how controversial it was. The final excerpt, from the *Daily Press* of Newport News, Virginia, reflects the opinion of many at the time (and also offers quite-different estimates for distances and the weight of the lighthouse).

The Light House Board's "Instructions to Light-Keepers," July 1881

The following Instructions are published for the guidance of light-keepers. They are required to read them carefully and attentively, and to refer to them whenever they have any doubts in regard to their duties or the manner of performing them....

1. The keeper is responsible for the care and management of the light, and for the station in general. He must enforce a careful attention to duty on the part of his assistants; and the assistants are strictly enjoined to render prompt obedience to his lawful orders.

2. In the absence of the keeper his duties will devolve upon the assistant present who is next in rank....

4. ... The keeper on watch must remain in the watchroom and give continuous attention to the light while he is on duty. When there is no assistant, the keeper must visit the light at least twice during the night between 8 P.M. and sunrise; and on stormy nights the light must be constantly looked after.

8. All keepers must acquaint themselves with the workings of the apparatus in their charge. Upon any doubtful point questions must be asked. When the station is visited by an officer or employee of the Light-House Establishment, especially while the machinist or lampist is there, the keepers must take pains to acquire knowledge of every detail regarding the mechanism of the apparatus. Ignorance upon any point will not be considered as an excuse for neglect of duty.

11. A light-house must never be left wholly unattended. Where there is a keeper and one or more assistants, either the keeper or

one of the assistants must be present. If there is only one keeper, some member of his family, or other responsible person, must be at the station in his absence.

16. Keepers must be courteous and polite to all visitors who conform to the regulations, and show them everything of interest about the station at such times as it will not interfere with their light-house duties. Keepers must not allow visitors to handle the apparatus or deface light-house property. Special care must be taken to prevent the scratching of names or initials on the glass of the lanterns or on the windows of the towers. No visitor should be admitted to the tower unless attended by a keeper.

17. Keepers must under no circumstances allow an intoxicated person to enter a light-tower, nor to remain on the premises longer than is necessary to get him away by the employment of all proper and reasonable means.

20. Keepers must make no change in the color of towers or buildings without written orders.

21. The utmost neatness of buildings and premises is demanded. Bedrooms, as well as other parts of the dwelling, must be neatly kept. Untidiness will be strongly reprehended; and its continuance will subject a keeper to dismissal.

208. The following recipe for whitewashing has been found by experience to answer on wood, brick, and stone, nearly as well as oil paint, and is much cheaper:

Slake half a bushel of unslaked lime with boiling water, keeping it covered during the process. Strain it and add a peck of salt, dissolved in warm water; three pounds of ground rice put in boiling water, and boiled to a thin paste; half a pound of powdered Spanish whiting, and a pound of clear glue, dissolved in warm water; mix these well together, and let the mixture stand for several days. Keep the wash thus prepared in a kettle or portable furnace, and when used put it on as hot as possible, with painters' or whitewash brushes.[1]

Orlandah Phillips on the early days at the Cape Lookout Lighthouse

This Mason, which was my great grandfather [probably Manaen Washington Mason, keeper at Cape Lookout from 1869 to 1876]…got appointed as lighthouse keeper. And at that day and time, the lighthouse was not run with electric bulbs and timing devices. It was run with lamps, with wicks, burning whale oil. And these granddaughters of his would come over in pairs…to help him tend the lights, and I'll proceed with that a little further. I've heard my grandmother tell tales about this. She said, in the fall of the year when it became stormy, that usually she and sister…they would carry up the salt and pepper and biscuits on a stormy night, and the little birds flying south would break their necks and wings against the light. They'd go out and gather 'em up, bring 'em in and clean 'em and stick 'em on a fork to hold 'em up to the wicks of the lighthouse light and roast 'em. She said that was things they looked forward to every fall that they had those birds, and invariably it happened.…Aunt Charlotte and grandmammy Ruffin, they'd tend the light in pairs, and incidentally, the light of course had the glass outside. I don't know w'er they had any prism or not, probably didn't, but they actually had cans of whale oil with a wick in it. And their job was to keep that wick clean and keep it full of oil, and they sat inside of the light.[2]

Cape Lookout Lighthouse
U.S. Coast Guard Archive

New York Times account of the August 7, 1918, sinking of the Diamond Shoals Lightship

Destruction by a submarine of the Diamond Shoals Lightship 71, a helpless craft anchored off Cape Hatteras to warn shipping from the treacherous shoals forming the "graveyard of the Atlantic Coast," confirms the belief of naval officials that German sea wolves sent to this side of the Atlantic are under orders to handicap commerce in all ways possible without exposing themselves to naval or other formidable opponents.

News of the shelling and sinking of the lightship came to the Navy Department today, clearing up the mystery of earlier reports from coast guard stations on the North Carolina coast that heavy shelling was heard at sea yesterday afternoon. The crew of twelve men on the lightship escaped in a small boat and rowed the ten or twelve miles to shore.

Subsequently the submarine appeared within half a mile of the land which projects far out from the main coast of North Carolina. There were no reports of attacks on villages, coast guard stations or lighthouses, and the purpose of the submarine commander in showing himself so near the beach was not clear....

Attacks on other vessels in that vicinity are to be expected, but naval patrol boats and seaplanes already are endeavoring to protect shipping and hunt out and destroy the enemy. With a long shore line on which to operate and deep water for submerging to hide from patrols, however, the advantage in this game of hide and seek lies with the enemy.[3]

William Tate recalls his days as a lighthouse inspector

There wasn't anybody up and down [Currituck] beach for 50 miles. In those days, there was just nothing on that beach....

They had a little store up at Corolla at that time. Mr. Johnny Austin ran the store. You probably had half a dozen Coca Colas. And [a] few items there. I'd go up to visit him for a while, while the [lighthouse] batteries were charging. They had a room there [in the lighthouse] that had enough rags to clean that place up for a hundred years. I had them all spread out nice on that bench, and that was a nice place to sleep. I had to stay there eight hours, and remember it took an hour to get across the sound and an hour to get back, so that was a 10-hour day. I saw no need wasting all that time. So I did a little bit of sleeping....

...If they decided to lay you off, they laid you off and hired you back a short while afterwards if they need you. In other words, you worked for the government when they needed you—not when you needed the job.[4]

Ben Dixon MacNeill on the engineering of the Cape Hatteras Lighthouse

About a hundred inhabitants of the Islands had jobs on the new lighthouse, and such of them as could qualify as bricklayers got the preposterously high wage of $1.50 per day, working from "can to can't," which is the vernacular for dawn to dusk. From kilns along the James River in Virginia scows brought 1,250,000 brick....

Earnest and helplessly superior young ensigns, and even sedate commanders, all of them instructed in the newer engineering practices in the best schools, look now with sometimes not quite urbane disbelief when any Islander, native or not, explains to them how the massive tower was designed and built. Its walls at the base are fourteen feet solid masonry, for one thing, and narrow to eight feet at the top. That, they will say, is rather wasteful, isn't it, when a little steel would have served admirably to give the tower strength, and they do not remember, if they ever knew, that Sir Henry Bessemer was only forty-four years old when the tower was designed and his manner of making steel had yet to find acceptance and use in America.

And the piling, now, they will inquire. There must be some massive piling under so formidable a structure....Tell them now about the piling, how many pieces of it and how deep into the earth was it driven?

There is no piling under the Lighthouse....

No piling. Perhaps for the reason that there were no pile drivers. Or, as the Islanders will tell you, wisdom and engineering science was [*sic*] not invented by Seabees or ensigns or put together in colleges....

When they were finished with their building the Engineers had a distinction that had not, and has not, been matched in the world. Here was a brick tower, 196 feet from base sill to the top brick. The iron superstructure added another dozen feet, and the whole of it cost $155,000. Even now when these young engineers look at it, its height, its thickness of wall, its cast-iron stairway anchored in massive masonry, they hesitate to say whether they could do it and at what cost....

Cape Hatteras Lighthouse
U.S. Coast Guard Archive

After the walls were finished they were painted and there was, as the Islander remembers with remote glee, a confusion in the design. Somebody somewhere got the papers mixed up, and the spiral striping that was intended for a new light tower fifty miles southwest on Cape Lookout was applied to the new Cape Hatteras tower, and the diamond-shaped figures, suitable for warning traffic away from Diamond Shoals, went to Lookout. It is still so. Tourists call it the Big Barber Pole and point their cameras at it. The Islanders have no such facetious name—it is The Lighthouse.[5]

"Cape Hatteras Lighthouse As I Knew It," by Rany Jennett

The lamp was lit one half hour before sunset and extinguished at sunrise. A kerosene-burning mantle lamp was the prime source of light. A vapor light, this was located in the center of a first order Fresnel lens which was about twelve feet in height and about six feet in diameter, and structured with over a thousand pieces of heavy glass prisms and bull's-eyes....The light was visible from twenty or twenty-five miles at sea....Close up, its twenty-four sheets of light were visible at the same time and gave the appearance of a giant lighted fan revolving slowly from the top of the tower.

Kerosene for the lamp had to be carried to the top of the lighthouse tower by hand in five-gallon cans. Clockworks had to be oiled and lenses inspected for smudges or spots and cleaned. Touching the lens with fingers was never allowed. The lenses were cleaned with alcohol every thirty days, and with powdered rouge [jeweler's polish], using a camel's hair brush, each six months.

The clock mechanism that powered the rotation of the lens operated much like the old grandfather clock. Weights attached to a cable, riding on a circular track, descended through the center of the lighthouse, wound around a steel drum beneath a train of clock-type gears, in mesh with a platform on which the lenses were mounted. The complete mechanism was locked in place by a brake. When the brake was released, the weights began their descent, rotating the drum, actuating movement to the great train, and thus revolving the lenses.

...Any variation in speed would alter the sequence of the light and confound the seamen aboard ship off the shoals, who identified each lighthouse by the pattern of its signals from the ship's charts. Using a stopwatch, the keeper on duty would time the rotation several times each watch....

Sometimes the lighthouse would need to be given a complete painting, and sometimes just a touch-up. Touching up was usually done by the keepers. A bo'sun chair would be rigged from the rail of the tower with a block and tackle, and one keeper would swing out on the side of the structure. The other two keepers would man the lead line to move him up or down.

A complete painting required a different arrangement. A paint box about twenty feet long by six feet wide, with a four-foot rail, would be used. This box was built to conform to the contour of the circular lighthouse, and would accommodate four people. My father would raise and lower this box by tying the lead line to the bumper of his car. If the painters needed to be raised, he would move forward, and if they needed to be lowered, he would go in reverse.

I remember on one occasion four local young fellows were hired to paint the lighthouse. In a short while they were carrying on in a playful manner and not paying much attention to the job at hand. There was white paint in the black areas and black on white in other places. Since these young men were acting up and out of the norm, my father suspected they must have brought some spirits with them or maybe even have tapped the alcohol at the top of the lighthouse, used to clean the lens. Being a man of even temperament and never verbally abusive, he let his actions speak to the problem at hand. Without saying a word, he entered the car, started the engine, and shifted into reverse, at a fast clip for about forty feet. Of course, this dropped the box and its occupants about fifty feet, with a sudden shocking halt to the whole operation. They started screaming and hollering, wanting to know, "Captain, what in the hell is going on?" Then he started lowering the box to the ground, and as they staggered out one by one, he said, "Go to the beach, take a swim, come back sober, and then go back to work." This they did, and their performance was quality. No hard feelings or bitterness, and no one was fired or quit his job....

Growing up at the lighthouse provided me with many good childhood memories. The three families at the lighthouse were, for the most part, quite large, and a mile south of the lighthouse at the Life Saving Station, there were four or five families. Visits were frequent between these neighbors. There have been words written to the effect that lighthouse keepers and their families had a very lonely life; however, we did not have this experience. In fact, just the opposite would be more apt to apply. The lighthouse has always been a favorite place to visit by the village folk so we would have lots of company, especially on Sunday afternoons and the evening hours, when the heat of summer was unbearable in the wooded areas of the villages. Swimming, baseball games, croquet, chasing wild horses and penning them in the yards for breaking to the saddle, and climbing the lighthouse were all a big part of our lives.

As often as I could, I would make the trip to the top with my father and help with some of the routine maintenance. I shined lots of brass in my young days at the lighthouse. This was not without some reward, however. My father would let me take the powerful spy glasses or binoculars and look at passing ships, so close to shore you would see sailors walking on the deck. Shipping lanes were closer to shore then than now....

Lighthouse young folks had an advantage over the village youngsters, in that a portable library was located at the principal keeper's house for use by lighthouse families. This contained books of all description and was furnished by the Lighthouse

Department. This library was in rotation with other lighthouses, used for six months, then sent to another lighthouse and replaced by another completely different selection of books. The Lighthouse Department had about six hundred of these libraries that were furnished to lighthouses throughout the country. As a result, these families were exposed to around two hundred books each year....

My childhood memories take me back to many pleasant happenings that could only be true for a youngster growing up under the shadow of such a magnificent and well-known guardian of seamen everywhere as the Cape Hatteras Lighthouse. The freedom that could only be afforded by the wide and long expanse of sandy beach and Atlantic Ocean was mine. This sea of blue-green water with its river of ink blue warm water flowing from south to north, named the Gulf Stream, could be as peaceful as a pond and as turbulent as the fury expressed by a woman scorned....

Climbing the lighthouse at every opportunity, up and down the steps, and even sneaking a slide down the rail on the lower levels (this, of course, was frowned on by the elders), walking to the top with string and old rags, going out on deck with makeshift parachutes and tossing them over to float gently to the ground or into the ocean. Ah, memories...

The outdoor privy was located over the big pond behind our house. It seemed that most any time you could see large snapping turtles swimming around the toilet. I would fashion a string and bent straight pin into a hook, with a piece of meat for bait. I would drop this fishing rig through one of the holes and hook me a turtle, let him struggle for a while and then let him go. One day, while I was busy hooking turtles in the old privy, my baby sister, who was about two, poked her head in the door, and asked, "What you doing, Rany, hooking turtles?" I said, "GO AWAY!" She asked, "Can I watch?" and before I could stop her, she had her head stuck in one of the smaller holes and could not get it back out. Needless to say, I became concerned and frightened, and ran to get my father who came and rescued baby....

Needless to say, I enjoyed my young life at the Cape Hatteras Lighthouse and the good memories of that life. Writing this has energized the computer in my mind and when the right button was pressed, all these things came back about what had happened over a span of almost seventy years.

The good times and further memories of life at Cape Hatteras Lighthouse came to an end in September, 1933. In late August of that year a severe storm hit the coast of North Carolina with not too much damage, and as we had experienced storms of this magnitude before, not too much concern was expressed. We'd had a very dry summer that year and the ponds surrounding the area were bone dry and the bottom even cracked, like a desert. The storm hit and the surging seas came rolling across the broad, flat beach. The empty ponds were able to take care of the overwash, and in a little while things were beginning to look normal again. However, the worst was yet to come. My father received word via telephone from down south that a real severe storm (we didn't call them hurricanes then) was moving up the coast packing winds of one hundred miles per hour, and would hit Hatteras Island full force. He knew this storm could be a killer and most especially so, since we had not fully recovered from the previous one a few weeks earlier. He moved us to the village of Buxton and instructed the two assistant keepers to do the same with their families. The three keepers stayed with their station. Lighthouse keepers could not leave their responsibility behind for any reason, even if their lives were in jeopardy. Immediate dismissal would be the result.

This storm proved to be as expected, and damage was severe, especially to the lower floors and furnishings. The sea busted down the door in our house and even turned a large, round, oak dining room table bottom up. Everything was one big mess. Some livestock drowned along the outer banks. Of course, back then, you could not see much physical damage along the beach because there was not anything such as buildings, only a Life Saving Station every seven miles.

There were six inlets cut along the Carolina coast during these two storms, two on Hatteras Island. We never returned to the lighthouse quarters again, but to each of us, it was always home, and still is to this day.[6]

"Let Lighthouse Go," December 20, 1989

After years of dickering over how to save the historic Cape Hatteras lighthouse, the National Park Service announced this week that it would move the structure inland about 500 feet to protect it from the advancing tides of the Atlantic Ocean.

There's no timetable for the move and no money available, so no one's sure when the 2,800-ton structure will be placed on rails and rolled inland. Hopefully it will be long enough for the park service, and those in Washington who control the agency's budget, to realize that moving the lighthouse is not a very bright idea.

For starters, the cost is prohibitive. It's estimated that the feat could run about $4.6 million. While the light is still used by the Coast Guard, it can hardly be considered a necessity with all the advanced navigational equipment that's available to ship captains and boaters. And, despite assurances from engineering experts, it's hard to believe that the 208-foot-tall brick structure, built 119 years ago, can be moved without toppling it.

The Cape Hatteras lighthouse has served for more than a century as a warning of coastal dangers. It also has become a popular tourist attraction. But erosion has eaten away more than 1,300 feet of shoreline in front of the lighthouse, putting it within 160 feet of the churning waves.

When the money, needs and risks are tallied, there's no way to justify heroic efforts to save the structure. It should be left to the tides and time. Nature should decide the fate of the lighthouse, not the park service.[7]

Cape Hatteras Lighthouse on its slow move toward the new inland relocation site in 1999
Courtesy of National Park Service

The Lifesaving Stations

What was arguably the most heroic period in Outer Banks history lasted a surprisingly short time.

In 1790, Secretary of the Treasury Alexander Hamilton established the Revenue Marine to aid in the collection of duties on shipped goods. By the late 1830s, it evolved a rescue component. The 1870s finally saw the creation of the United States Lifesaving Service and its express mission to aid those in peril at sea.

The Outer Banks had as great a need for such service as any section of the American coast. Cape Hatteras juts into the Atlantic at the intersection of the south-flowing, cold-water Labrador Current and the north-flowing, warm-water Gulf Stream. The collision of waters in the area dubbed "the Graveyard of the Atlantic" has played havoc with shipping for centuries.

In 1874, Congress designated funds for seven Outer Banks lifesaving stations, stretching from Currituck Beach southward to Little Kinnakeet, north of Buxton. Four years later, another eleven stations were funded, the plan being to space them roughly seven miles apart all the way down the Banks.

The cash-paying jobs at the stations were highly coveted in a land of need. Although the early years saw some political appointments of men with no particular skill in lifesaving, the level of professionalism quickly rose. District supervisors are said to have worn white gloves during inspections. One keeper had his underlings sit at meals in the same alignment in which they manned their surfboat. One surfman was supposedly let go because he couldn't see a bird atop a telephone pole some distance away.

Meanwhile, the stations grew into social centers. People came for water during dry times, as the stations had the best local cisterns. They came for shelter during storms, and to watch the surfmen train on the beach.

It was a fact of the profession that lifesavers were most likely to have to risk their lives during the worst possible weather. In the immortal words of Patrick Etheridge, keeper of the Creeds Hill and Cape Hatteras stations, "The Blue Book [the lifesavers' manual] says we've got to go out and it doesn't say a damn thing about having to come back."[1]

Crew from Chicamacomico Life-Saving Station launching a Dobbins lifeboat
Courtesy of North Carolina Sea Grant

In 1915, the Lifesaving Service was folded into the United States Coast Guard, which has the dual responsibilities of enforcement and rescue. The lifesaving stations began to be phased out after that point. The surviving stations are treasured today, some having been converted to other uses and a few serving as museums.

The first excerpt below predates the Lifesaving Service and shows the competing mindsets on the Outer Banks. On one hand, residents were highly sympathetic toward, and protective of, victims at sea, many having descended from shipwreck survivors themselves. On the other hand, some of their brethren profited from, and even instigated, shipwrecks, the use and reselling of wrecked goods being almost an economic necessity. The residents' better angels thus had to conquer this latter impulse in order to grow a lifesaving culture devoted to selflessness and sacrifice.

The second excerpt details the wreck of the *Metropolis* off Currituck Beach in late January 1878. The *Metropolis*, a former naval vessel that had participated in the Battle of Roanoke Island in 1862, was by then a decrepit freighter. On its final voyage, shifting cargo caused it to take on water, which overwhelmed the pumps and then the engines. It drifted powerless until hitting the shoals just a hundred yards off Currituck Beach. Officially, eighty-five people died. The wreck followed by two months the sinking of the *Huron* twenty miles south, in which ninety-eight souls perished. Together, the two disasters brought heavy criticism of Congress for underfunding the Lifesaving Service, which led to the appropriations for the second group of Outer Banks stations that same year.

The third excerpt consists of logbook entries from the famous Pea Island Life-Saving Station, located near the northern end of Hatteras Island. Pea Island was the nation's first station with an all-black crew, and also the first to have an African-American commanding officer, Richard Etheridge, born a slave in 1842. The entries suggest the range of operations performed by the lifesavers. The stations are widely understood to have focused eastward, toward vessels in the Atlantic. But it is interesting to note how often the Pea Island men had to hustle westward across the island to help those in trouble on Pamlico Sound.

Shipwreck survivors realized their good fortune in falling into the hands of the Outer Banks lifesavers. The fourth excerpt is a thank-you penned by men of the *Florence E. Magee,* rescued by the Bodie Island crew in 1896. The survivors continued to be "succored" at the station—in the parlance of the time—for the better part of a week after the date of their letter.

The final excerpt is Captain John Allen Midgett's recounting of the signature rescue in the history of the Outer Banks stations—that of the British tanker *Mirlo* during World War I. The *Mirlo*, bearing a cargo of petroleum, was seven miles off the Chicamacomico station (by then operating under the Coast Guard umbrella) when it was either torpedoed by a German submarine or struck a mine. The British captain turned west but made it only a short distance before the *Mirlo* exploded. Captain Midgett and the Chicamacomico men spent thirty minutes trying to launch through heavy surf, then confronted a wall of flames when their small boat finally reached the site of the disaster. They ultimately rescued forty-two sailors of the *Mirlo*, for which they were each awarded the Gold Lifesaving Medal from the United States and the Victory Medal from Britain.

A *Harper's* writer assesses the state of affairs in 1860

A wilder country than the Banks can not well be imagined. Where it widens to four or five miles there is a little tillage; but, generally speaking, nature has but few encroachments on her primeval rule to complain of. The men may be sweepingly described as combining the vocations of farming, fishing, and wrecking. Their ideas of meam and teem have been accused of some slight confusion on the subject of stranded property…Their kindness and hospitality to wrecked seamen is unfailing and unlimited. Instances have been told us of the surrender, for weeks together, of a shoreman's whole house to a company of such unfortunates without the prospect of compensation.

Formerly, practices were attributed to a portion of the Bankers slightly inconsistent with this description. Nags Head derives its name, according to the prevalent etymology, from an old device employed to lure vessels to destruction. A Banks pony was driven up and down the beach at night, with a lantern tied around his neck. The up-and-down motion resembling that of a vessel, the unsuspecting tar would steer for it. Other means of increasing the wreck harvest were resorted to. But the march of moral improvement, let us hope, has abolished them all….

Our own impression is, that Bankers may be found…who make more money out of wrecks, of one kind or another, and are every way less to be trusted than those of Arabia.[2]

Special dispatch to the *New York Times* regarding the wreck of the *Metropolis*, January 31, 1878

During the south-east gale this afternoon the steamship *Metropolis*, of New York, from Philadelphia for Para, South America, with stores and laborers on board, grounded on the outer bar off Currituck Beach, about three miles south of the light, and 10 miles north of Kitty Hawk Signal Station. She at once bilged and floated broadside to the sea. Fifty of the passengers and crew got on shore, and the rest, about 150 in number, were lost, no assistance being rendered from the shore, from life stations, or fishermen….

One of the men saved states that all last night the vessel encountered heavy weather, with a strong gale from south-east. About 6:30 this evening the ship struck, when all was confusion on board, the sea making a complete breach over the vessel, washing the passengers and crew into the seething foam. Amid the howling of the tempest and the roaring of the surf, the orders of the officers could not be heard. When the vessel struck, several of her boats were swept from the decks. Those who reached the shore, managed to do so by holding on to pieces of the wreck....

No assistance was given to the wreck by the signal stations or by the life saving crew in the vicinity.[3]

Pea Island Life-Saving Station was unique in that it was manned by an all-black crew. The station continued to be manned by African-American Coast Guardsmen until it was deactivated in 1947.
Courtesy of U.S. Coast Guard

Excerpts from the log of the Pea Island station

Date: November 30, 1879, Vessel: *M & E Henderson*, Cargo: Phosphate Rock

On the 30th of November, 1879, patrolman Tillett, who had the morning watch on the beat south, returned to the [station]

house a few minutes after five o'clock in the morning[,] lit a fire in the stove and called the cook, then went up-stairs, and looking with the marine glass from the south window, perceived, at some distance in the clear moonlight, a man whom he at first thought was a fisherman. Presently noticing that the man was without a hat[,] it at once occurred to him that he might have been washed ashore from a wreck. He immediately aroused the keeper and crew, and started out in advance, [and] soon came up to a haggard and dripping figure, a sailor, tottering along very much exhausted, and only able to articulate, ["C]aptain drowned[,] masts gone.["] Debris from the wreck came ashore just a mile and [a] quarter south of the Station.

Date: October 5, [1881,] Vessel: *Thomas J. Lancaster*, Cargo: Ice

Pea Island crew assisted the Chicamacomico crew[,] which was first on the scene. Thirteen people on the wreck. More than 28 hours after the vessel grounded, the life-savers brought 6 survivors safely to shore. The Captain[,] three of his younger daughters and three of the crew drowned. Two of the survivors, the Captain's wife and one daughter, had been tied to the rigging to prevent their being washed overboard. They remained in the rigging for twenty-four hours before being rescued.

Date: January 9, 1884, Vessel: *Excel*, Cargo: Mail

The sail-boat *Excel*, employed in carrying the mail between Manteo and Kinnakeet[,] was caught in Pamlico Sound, on the 5th, by a violent snow storm, and the occupant of the boat compelled to leave his craft about a mile from Pea Island Station and to seek refuge at that station. But for the shelter afforded him he must have perished. The storm continued until the night of the 9th, when the wind changed suddenly to a strong gale from the southwest. The boat being deeply laden sank at midnight, and the contents were washed overboard.

The crew of the station reached the boat early on the morning of the 10th and succeeded in raising it and bringing it to the shore. They also recovered about two-thirds of the cargo, and after putting it on board, saw the boat safely to its destination. The man was at the station five days.

Date: May 15, 1887, Body Found

In the morning the keeper of the Pea Island Station found the body of a drowned man about a mile south of the station. The head and face were badly disfigured, and there were no marks by which the remains could be identified[. A] leather wallet in one of the trousers pockets contained a small amount of money. With the assistance of the Keeper of the Oregon Inlet Station the body was decently interred.

Date: April 24, 1889, Body Found

A surfman of the Pea Island Station while patrolling the beach observed a dead body in the surf, which proved to be that of a young colored sailor. It was pulled out on the beach clear of the tide, and the keeper was notified. The clothing was thoroughly searched[. I]n the pockets were found several papers and twenty-five dollars in currency. From the papers it was learned that the name of the deceased was Robert Nolan, aged seventeen years[,] and that he had served on the English ship *Canute* and the American ship *David Crocket* [*sic*]. The letters on the cork jacket which he wore were so nearly obliterated that the name of the vessel from which he had been lost could not be ascertained. The money and papers were turned over to the proper authorities and the body was decently buried.

Date: October 11, 1896, Vessel: *E. S. Newman*

Sails blown away and master obliged to beach her during hurricane 2 miles below station at 7 P.M. Signal of distress was immediately answered by patrolman's Coston light. Keeper and crew quickly started for the wreck with beach apparatus. The sea was sweeping over the beach and threatened to prevent reaching scene of disaster, but they finally gained a point near the wreck. It was found to be impossible to bury the sand anchor (for the breeches buoy), as the tide was rushing over the entire beach, and they decided to tie a large-sized shot line around two surfmen and send them down through the surf as near the vessel as practicable. These men waded in and succeeded in throwing a line on board with the heaving stick. It was made fast to the master's three-year-old child, who was then hauled off by the surfmen and carried ashore. In like manner his wife and the seven men composing the crew were rescued under great difficulties and with imminent peril to the life-savers. They were all taken to station and furnished with food and clothing, and during [the] next three days the surfmen aided in saving baggage and stores from wreck. On the 14th three of the crew left for Norfolk and on the 21st the remainder departed for their homes, the vessel having proved a total loss.

Date: April 14, 1903, Vessel: *Topaz*, Cargo: Eggs and Barrels

Capsized in a squall off Rollinson's Reef 5 miles WNW of station (in Pamlico Sound) at 4 P.M. The life-saving crew pulled to the vessel, but finding no one on board, returned to station. The next morning, accompanied by the surfmen from New Inlet station, they assisted in righting, bailing out, and temporarily repairing the capsized craft.

Date: December 11, 1904, Vessel: *Montana*, Cargo: Salt

Shortly before midnight, during a heavy NNW gale with thick snowstorm and rough sea, the *Montana*, a three mastered [masted] schooner laden with salt and carrying a crew of seven, all told, struck the beach ¼ mile N of station and 300 yards from shore. Heavy seas swept over her, and the crew, after burning a torch for help, took refuge in the forerigging[. T]he N patrol promptly reported the disaster, and keeper and crew, provided with beach apparatus, reached the shore abreast of the wreck at 12:10 A.M., the keeper having telephoned for assistance to Oregon Inlet and New Inlet stations, the former crew arriving at 1 A.M. and the latter some time later. It was impossible to launch a boat through the heavy surf, and after lighting a bonfire the life-savers placed the wreck gun and fired several lines, some of them going adrift and some to the wreck, but none in such position that the shipwrecked crew could reach it. At daylight the surfmen laid a line over the spring stay, which the crew succeeded in reaching, and after several hours of difficult work six men were landed. The seventh man, the ship's cook, being of advanced year, was washed overboard during the night and lost. Four of the rescued men were sheltered at the station for eleven days, and two for sixteen days. The *Montana* became a total wreck, and was sold by the master for a small sum.

Date: February 13, 1906, Vessel: *Jennie Lockwood*

During a severe northerly gale, thick weather, and high seas this vessel stranded at 5 A.M. 200 yards E of the station. The patrol discovered her and reported her to the keeper, who telephoned to the Oregon Inlet station to come down and lend a hand at the wreck. At 10 A.M. the Pea Island crew arrived abreast of the stranded craft with their beach apparatus and fired a shot from the Lyle gun, the line falling over the fore rigging. The crew from Oregon Inlet now arrived, and by means of the breeches buoy all hands—there were 7 in all—were safely landed and taken to the Pea Island station and succored for six days. The schooner was lost.[4]

Testimonial from the crew of the
Florence E. Magee

Bodie Island, North Carolina
February 28, 1894

To Whom It May Concern:

We, the undersigned, master and mariners of the schooner *Florence E. Magee*, wrecked on this beach on the night of the 25th instant, desire to testify to the great bravery and exertion exhibited by Captain Jesse T. Etheridge and his gallant crew of Life-Saving Station No. 15 [Bodie Island] in rescuing us from our perilous position on the wreck. They worked from the time the wreck was discovered, at 12:40 A.M. the 26th, until 4 P.M., when we were landed. Having used every effort to shoot a line across the wreck, and succeeding in this, [the lifesavers] found it impossible to land us on account of the long distance the vessel was stranded from the beach; [Captain Etheridge] launched the surfboat, and at great peril of his life and crew came to us and rescued us. For this rescue and the efforts put forth to accomplish it we desire to express in this matter our appreciation of his kindness in rescuing us and the very kind treatment which we have received during our stay at the station.

Yours, truly,
Henry C. Rogers, Master; Samuel G. Black; [and eight others][5]

Captain John Allen Midgett's account of the
Mirlo rescue, August 16, 1918

At 4:30 P.M. lookout reported seeing a great mass of water shoot up in the air which seemed to cover the after portion of a steamer that was about seven miles E. by S. of this Station and heading in a Northerly direction[. A] great quantity of smoke rising from the after part of the Steamer was noticed but [the vessel] continu[ed] her course for a few minutes when she swung around for the beach and then head[ed] off shore[. T]he fire was now seen to shoot up from the stern of the Steamer and heavy explosions were heard. I called all hands including the liberty man and started with power Surfboat No. 1046[.] Wind N.E. moderate, heavy sea on beach, had difficulty in getting away from the beach, cleared the beach at about 5:00 P.M. and headed for the burning wreck, then about 5 miles off shore. I met one of the ship's boats with the captain and sixteen men in her; I was informed that their ship was a British tanker and that she was torpedoed which caused the loss of ship. I was informed that two other boats were in the vicinity of the burning gas and oil that was coming up from the sunken ship. I directed the captain of that boat where and how to go and wait my arrival, but not to attempt a landing as the sea was strong and there was danger of him capsizing his boat without assistance. I then headed for the burning gas and oil.

Surfmen who rescued the *Mirlo* crew. John Allen Midgett is on far left.
Courtesy of U.S. Coast Guard

On arrival I found the sea a mass of wreckage and burning gas and oil[. T]here were two great masses of flames... in places covered with the burning gas. And in between the two great flames at times when the smoke would clear away a little, a life boat could be seen bottom up[,] six men clinging to it, the heavy swell washing over the boat. With difficulty I ran our boat through the smoke, floating wreckage and burning gas and oil, and managed to rescue the six men from the burning sea. Who informed me that at times they had to dive under the water to save themselves from being burned to death[. A]ll had burns but none serious. They informed me that they were sure that there were no men afloat except those in the boats. But this did not stop our searching in the vicinity of the fire for those missing men, but no more men could be found. These six men seemed to know nothing of the other boats, they being lost sight of in the fire and great clouds of smoke that were rising from the burning gas and oil. I headed our boat before the sea and wind in hopes of finding the missing boat, and in a short time the 3rd which was the missing boat with nineteen men was sighted about nine miles S.E. of station. I ran alongside[,] took this boat in tow and proceeded to where I had directed the first boat to be[. T]his boat was soon reached and taken in tow. I had in station boat six men rescued from the bottom of overturned boat. And one of the boats being towed containing seventeen and the other boat containing nineteen[. T]he wind was beginning to freshen from the N.E. and sea rising on beach.

I was heading for my station when about two mile[s] South of station it began to get dark and for safety I decided to make a landing. I anchored the two ship's boats about six hundred yards from the beach and transferred the men to station boat, landing all in station boat at four trips, and then put surfmen in the two ship's boats and had them landed. As fast as the men were landed they were carried to the station by my team of horses and the horse from station No. 180 [the Gull Shoal Coast Guard Station]. The Keeper and crew from station No. 180 met me at the beach and assisted me in landing the crew. All boats including the station boat were pulled up on the beach out of danger of the sea. I landed last trip at 9:00 P.M. and arrived at station at 11:00 P.M., myself and crew very tired. I furnished the Captain and all his crew who needed it medical aid, and then with some dry clothing, and their supper, and with a place to sleep.[6]

The Hunt Clubs

In a brief span, nature created the bird-hunting grounds of the northern Outer Banks.

Even faster, humans nearly destroyed them.

Currituck Inlet shoaled over in 1823. Rivers continued to empty into Currituck Sound from the west, but ocean water no longer had a means of entry from the east. As the salinity of the water decreased, oyster beds died out and marsh grasses flourished. The grasses attracted ducks and geese to the sound, situated as it was on the Atlantic Flyway. During migrations, game birds turned the skies black.

Where quarry went, hunters followed. Sportsmen shot from "batteries"—blinds in which they lay on their backs, partially submerged and surrounded by floating decoys. Market hunters employed "punt guns"—ten-foot-long, boat-mounted shotguns that could kill a hundred ducks in a single volley. Meanwhile, the locks on the Albemarle and Chesapeake Canal—a waterway from Norfolk to Elizabeth City—were removed, which allowed Chesapeake Bay salt water to enter Currituck Sound, which began to kill the marsh grasses. The crowded skies started to clear.

Though the Currituck Shooting Club organized in 1857, the hunt clubs were mostly a Reconstruction-era phenomenon. Union soldiers returning home from the Civil War spoke of the abundant Currituck game. Wealthy Northerners investigated and found conditions to their liking. Among the members of the Currituck Shooting Club were Andrew Carnegie and J. P. Morgan; among those who hunted at the Whalehead Club were Dwight D. Eisenhower and Jack Dempsey. Ultimately, dozens of hunt clubs were clustered around Currituck Sound and southern Virginia's Back Bay.

Currituckers have long taken a beating from their "betters." Virginia surveyor and planter William Byrd had this to say in the early 1700s: "These People live so much upon Swine's flesh, that it...makes them likewise extremely hoggish in their Temper, and many of them seem to Grunt rather than Speak in their ordinary conversation."[1] The influx of Northern money after the Civil War opened the floodgates of Yankee superiority. "The idlers of the country—the young sawbones, half-fledged lawyers, small merchants, innkeepers, scions of old families run to seed, and the crowd usually found gathered about the post office or barroom, of the southern village—are a class of humans I do not admire," a *Forest & Stream* scribe wrote of Currituck mainlanders in 1881. "The taverns are characterized by dirt, fleas, bugs, greasy bad coffee, saucy darkey help and high prices."[2]

Insults aside, the newcomers were a boon to the local economy. Currituck Sound had never been suited to ports and shipping, given its average depth of five feet. And the changing salinity forced a transition from the locals' longtime dependence on harvesting oysters, shrimp, crabs, and clams. The hunt clubs stepped in to fill the void. Currituckers were hired to build clubhouses, to ferry Northerners to the islands, to cook and clean for them and tend to their daily needs, to serve as guides, and to care for the properties in the off-season.

And the best of the hunt-club set proved instrumental in saving the dwindling bird populations they had helped to create. The Lacy Act, enacted in 1900 to prohibit the sale of wildlife, effectively ended market hunting. And the clubs began regulating themselves. Bag limits—once twenty-five ducks and ten geese per man per day at the Currituck Shooting Club, for example—were reduced, then reduced again and again as necessary. Club members established hunting seasons and prohibited shooting on portions of their properties, thereby creating refuge areas. The foremost visionary and conservationist among them, Joseph Palmer Knapp, created an organization called More Game Birds in America, which became Ducks Unlimited.

Select hunt clubs remain in operation today, but the glory days are long past. The clubs' real legacy lies in Currituck National Wildlife Refuge and Mackay Island National Wildlife Refuge—and the abundant wildfowl that stop over on their migrations, to the pleasure of nature-loving visitors.

The first two excerpts below are an article on the creation of the Kitty Hawk Bay Sportsmen's Club and an homage to a memorable "Chesapeake dog" owned by that club. Both pieces are from *Forest & Stream*, a magazine that helped launch the National Audubon Society and that counted Theodore Roosevelt among its contributors. It later merged with *Field & Stream*.

The next piece concerns the Swan Island Club, founded by a party of New York hunters whose yacht grounded in Currituck Sound in 1870. They addressed their problem by buying the adjacent island; their yacht remained where it lay until burning in 1877. The Nature Conservancy purchased the property in 1977.

The fourth excerpt describes the latter days of the Whalehead Club. In 1922, Edward Collings Knight Jr. purchased the Lighthouse Club for his second wife, a hunter who was barred from membership in the other, all-male Currituck clubs. He dredged land along Currituck Sound to create a moat and a separate island, where he built a three-story French château featuring such amenities as an elevator and fresh and salt running water. During the Knights' eleven-year tenure, their "club" welcomed a maximum three guests at a time, and only twenty-five altogether. The property then passed to Ray Adams, who christened it the Whalehead Club. It subsequently served as a Coast Guard installation, a boarding school, and a facility for the testing of solid rocket fuel before being purchased by Currituck County in the 1990s and preserved as a waterfowl heritage museum. Located in Corolla in the shadow of the Currituck Beach Lighthouse, it is open for touring today.

Budding conservationist Joseph Palmer Knapp was the owner of Mackay Island, located between Bodie Island and the mainland at the Virginia border. The next piece discusses his foibles as a hunt-club proprietor and details some of his many charitable acts on behalf of Currituck residents.

The second-last excerpt concerns the most famous of the hunt clubs—the Currituck Shooting Club, located south of the Whalehead Club on Bodie Island, and not to be confused with the Currituck Gunning and Fishing Club on Mackay Island. Though the facilities were Spartan, clubhouse practices were anything but. Stock-market reports were delivered to the ultra-exclusive members by a butler bearing them on a silver tray. The first Southern member, Congressman Thurmond Chatham, was not admitted until ninety years after the club's founding. The institution's second clubhouse, listed on the National Register, burned in 2003.

The final excerpt, a portion of a North Carolina Supreme Court decision, summarizes a latter-day controversy involving one of the old hunt clubs. Earl F. Slick, both a conservationist and a developer, bought the Pine Island Club and its 1913-vintage clubhouse in 1973. Two years later, he installed a steel gate and an armed guard to block traffic access across his property to Corolla, to the north. The result was the near-complete isolation of the village, as vehicles weren't allowed through the Back Bay refuge above the Virginia line either. Though Slick donated much of his parcel to the National Audubon Society in 1979, a lease arrangement allowed him control over matters including access. The issue was fought out in the courts well into the 1980s, the locals ultimately winning free passage on what became a public thoroughfare.

Article in support of a Kitty Hawk hunt club, *Forest & Stream*, April 1881

The organization of the "Kitty Hawk Bay Sportsmen's Club" will be regarded by a large number of gentlemen sportsmen throughout America as a progressive and timely movement toward the preservation of our choicest varieties of wild fowl and the rarer species of game fish, which, if properly protected in the localities which they frequent during their migrations, would for many generations to come afford hunters and anglers rare sport, combined with opportunities for mental repose and bodily invigoration so much needed by the overworked in all our large cities.

The ruthless destruction of canvas back, redhead, black head and teal ducks in the waters of Currituck, Kitty Hawk Bay, North Carolina, during the month of October, 1880, by natives and market-shooters who employ batteries by day and fire by night, is a circumstance greatly to be deplored. During the period mentioned canvas back and redhead ducks were slaughtered by the thousands and packed in barrels, only to decompose before reaching market. Such a general and wanton destruction as this of our very choicest wildfowl is shocking to the sensibilities of every true sportsman, and cannot often be repeated without the most serious consequences.

It is plain that these shooting grounds must pass into the possession and control of well-managed club organizations, or a marked decrease and rapid extinction of game, now so abundant, will surely follow.

The various clubs heretofore organized in this section have found it difficult to secure legislation favorable to their interests, chiefly because the clubs themselves have owned comparatively little territory or shooting privileges. The Kitty Hawk Bay Club, owning as it does nearly fifty thousand acres of land and controlling a water frontage of over fifty miles, will, by reason of its vested rights, become a leading factor in obtaining such legislation as is now needed for the preservation and protection of game.... The distance from New York is now covered in about twenty-three hours instead of eighty hours as was formerly the case. The latter advantages will be greatly appreciated by members of the club living in New York, as they have rarely if ever before been combined with such unusual opportunities for really first-class shooting and fishing as are here offered....

We have ever deemed the question of game preservation one of national importance, and have felt a growing interest in this region, whose very remoteness and inaccessibility, rather than the intelligence of its people, have combined to protect and secure from extermination its vast, varied and almost number-less flocks.[3]

Forest & Stream describes a "favorite water dog"

The favorite water dog here is the Chesapeake dog, as they are strong, intelligent and faithful, and are unsurpassed retrievers. They are just the color of wild grass in shooting season. Wonderful stories are told of their sagacity. Some years ago Mr. Bodine, of New York city, a veteran sportsman, Col. Wilson Hollowell, of Pasquotank county in this State, and a Mr. Cadwell, of Currituck, were shooting canvas-backs on Morgan Island in Currituck Sound. Mr. Bodine went into a blind at the south end of the island, and as he was troubled with a tinge of rheumatism when exposed, Cadwell loaned him his Chesapeake bitch to bring in his birds. Col. Hollowell and Cadwell went to the north end of the island, about half a mile distant, and all three were soon hard at it and had good sport. It was very cold and the ice was very thick near the shore, and at last the bitch "Bonny" began to hang back when Mr. Bodine killed a bird, and it was only by speaking crossly to her that she would go into the water. After a while the dog disappeared after every shot, but soon came back bringing a canvas-back, and several times brought in two and laid them at the sportsman's feet. He continued firing all day, and when the sun went down launched his skiff and started to take in the other sportsmen. He picked up quite a number of ducks that Bonny had failed to bring in, and on counting found he had about two dozen more ducks than he was entitled to, judging from his count and the amount of ammunition he had fired away. He was puzzled to account for the overplus, but thought perchance shots had killed more than he had calculated. He soon reached the stands of Hollowell and Cadwell and they got their traps together to embark in the skiff. But when they looked for their game they discovered that their thirty odd canvas-backs had dwindled down to about a dozen. Cadwell had waded out in long boots on the shoals to round up the fowl as they were shot and had thrown them on the bank among the rushes. He began to swear, and abuse the unknown thief who had stolen his game. But when Mr. Bodine related his experience, and they called Bonny to account her sheepish and deprecating manner satisfied them who was the real thief. She had run across the island after every shot that Mr. Bodine fired, and stolen a duck from the pile of the other sportsmen to avoid going into the cold, icy water.

A descendant of this same bitch, by the same name, is famous as a retriever, and has been known to bring in three dead ducks at a time and to dive in deep water after crippled ducks and bring out two at a time. She will count the ducks as they fall, and will not rest satisfied until she brings them in when sent out. She recently had her first litter of pups, which sold readily for ten dollars each to the native gunners. Wreck, another celebrated bitch of Albemarle and Chesapeake stock mixed, has been known to swim one hundred yards out into the ocean during stormy weather and bring in a crippled beach bird. Both these dogs have been secured by the Kitty Hawk Club for breeding purposes.[4]

The largest single day's hunt at Swan Island, photographed by Moses Williams on November 11, 1901

Hortense Poyner Parkerson's memories of the Swan Island Club

Going home to Swan Island from the mainland of Knotts Island after sundown on a cold winter evening, I remember "Papa," my father, pushing the little skiff in which we sat, with a long pole. With each push our little family moved along silently over the sound, almost touching rafts of ducks and geese gliding along as one body, not appearing to notice our little boat. They covered the water like an old patchwork quilt—dark colored blocks of feathered hues sifting through the semidarkness.

And I remember the sounds. Unique music the ducks and geese made, an euphony of whistling swan notes blending into what "Papa" called "cathedral music." These feathered fluters did sound heavenly.

Yes, and I remember the sounds of sportsmans' [*sic*] guns as they shot from the many blinds on points of marsh around Swan Island: "pop! pop! pop! ba-room, ba-room! boom! boom! boom!" rang out when the wind was blowing chilling air across the marsh and ducks and geese were "flying."

I remember the busy bustling Swan Island Club when hunting season was in full swing. Wealthy sportsmen from Massachusetts arriving and departing...

The big clubhouse, I remember; starting at the cupola from which one could see the Atlantic, the sound, the lighthouse, Knotts Island and marshes....The clubroom stretched across the front of the clubhouse....One end of this room was used for dining. A big overstuffed sofa faced the huge fireplace where a Latin phrase was inscribed on a wooden board. The phrase which I don't recall was to the effect that of all places this was the most pleasant and enjoyable to those who were fortunate enough to come. I remember visits to this room when sportsmen were there and my father was invited for a "toddy" after a successful hunting day.

I remember John, the Negro butler and his wife Lizzie, the chief cook. John's pantry had shelves of white ironstone dishes and shining silver. I watched John clean the lamp chimneys of the many kerosene lamps and fill them from a tin oil can and a funnel. I could smell the coffee as he ground it for use. In memory I can see John's snaggled front tooth as he smiled and ate leftover broiled ducks returned to the kitchen after a sumptuous dinner in the clubroom.

I remember the "duckhouse" filled to its rafters with ducks, geese and swan (before the ban). They were "hung" before being shipped away or eaten in the clubhouse. In one end was a huge wicker basket for feathers when fowl was picked....

I remember the guides. Letters to my father from the sportsmen stipulated their choices. They had everything in readiness for the arrival of their "man." Shells, decoys, boats, guns, licenses, retrievers and more. Their success depended upon anticipating every eventuality and being prepared for it. Guides also chopped the wood and built the fires in the stoves that warmed each sportsman's room in early morning....I must add that guides were good "shots" and many times saved the sportsman's poor "shot" by supplementing a better one!

And lastly, I remember the tastes. Roasted Canvas Backs, broiled Teal, fried "shore birds" in wine gravy, and baked ham. Ginger bread, fried perch caught on hook and line, cornbread and fresh corn on the cob—fried soft crabs—these tastes I remember. Long ago at Swan Island Club in the Currituck Sound of North Carolina life was "different."[5]

Travis Morris's "Recollections of Whalehead Club during the 1940s"

I believe it was 1939 when Mr. Lindsay Warren was congressman from this district. Daddy got a letter from him asking...to take Mr. Ray Adams, who was a meat packer from Washington D.C., up the beach and show him the Whalehead Club. It was Adams who bought the place and named it the Whalehead Club in 1940.

I remember going to that clubhouse the first time. All the furniture was normally covered with white sheets, but was uncovered for Mr. Adams's inspection. I remember a grand piano, two grandfather clocks and a safe with ducks and other wildlife on it that had come from the old Light House Club. The dining room had a long table and a long buffet. I remember a bellows by one of the fireplaces, a leather couch and pretty chandeliers....

As a young boy I went duck hunting with Daddy at Whalehead Club on several occasions. There were usually a lot of people there, and most were either senators or congressmen or Coast Guard admirals. On the afternoon of the hunt, we would go to Poplar Branch Landing to meet the boat. Whalehead, Currituck and Pine Island Clubs all left from Poplar Branch Landing....

The Whalehead Club circa 1925

It was about six miles across and up Currituck Sound from Poplar Branch to Corolla. When we got to Whalehead, it would be getting late in the afternoon, and there would usually be a big bunch of canvasback out by the end of the point as we headed in the channel to the club. Mr. Adams fed ducks there without hunting them so people could see them from the big picture windows in the living room. When we docked in the basin, somebody would be there with an old army truck to take the bags up to the house. There was a command car for guests to ride in.

When we got inside the house, there were roaring oak fires in the fireplaces. After everybody settled in their rooms, the men had drinks and it would soon be time for dinner. Afterward, the men sat around to spin yarns until bedtime. By 8:30 P.M. Mr. Adams would tell his guests to stay up as long as they wanted to, but he was going to bed....At about 5:00 A.M., somebody knocked on the door and told us it was time to get up.

After breakfast we walked to the dock in front of the club. The guides had tied several skiffs behind each gas boat and dropped them off at various blinds. At lunchtime the gas boats came by to pick everybody up for lunch. After lunch and usually a nap, we went back out to hunt until take up time at 4:20 P.M. I saw as many as one hundred ducks and geese at the game room in the boathouse.[6]

"History of Mackay Island," by Melinda Lukei

In 1917 John L. Roper Lumber Co. sold the land for $25,000 to Thomas Dixon and Harriett his wife after all the timber had been cut. This land included 2,500 acres of Mackay Island, Bellows Bay and Bucks Island in the Currituck Sound. Thomas Dixon was a romantic novel writer of the reconstruction period. He wrote a book *The Clansman*, that was made into a movie *Birth of a Nation* in 1915 directed by D. W. Griffith, which marked the beginning of modern movie making.

Mr. Joseph Palmer Knapp started coming to Knotts Island with Mr. Dixon during hunting season. He was a native of Brooklyn, New York. On 31 Dec. 1918 Thomas Dixon from New York sold Mackay Island to Joseph Knapp for $39,211....Mr. Knapp bought the land of Mackay Island for a hunting retreat. He was publisher for *Collier's Magazine*. He was an executive in Crowell Enterprises. His father was founder of the Metropolitan Insurance Company. He managed it after he inherited the stock....He had an apartment in the River House in New York, a home in the Catskills and a camp in Canada. He also helped establish the colleges and universities of North

Carolina through his generous donations....Mr. Knapp built a three story southern mansion including gardens, servants' quarters, and a swimming pool in the shape of Knotts Island. The pool was built and filled with salt water so he wouldn't have to take his wife to Virginia Beach. Many of the plants in Mrs. Knapp's garden were shipped in from all over the world.

Mr. Knapp hired about thirty local people to be his gardeners, guides, maids, butlers, and drivers. During the hard times on Knotts Island Mr. Knapp hired as many as sixty persons and paid them $60.00 a month which was a lot of money to the people in this area. He stocked the Island with pheasants, quail, deer and started a farm stocked with cattle, hogs and poultry. He bought 250 quail to add to the Island, and 500 Mongolian Pheasants. 5,000 ducks were raised each year under a brooder. He turned these birds loose to breed and make game for himself. He planted buckwheat and milo maize for the birds to feed on. He shot two of the pheasants and said he couldn't shoot anything that beautiful again. Only the foxes and raccoons killed the pheasants after that.

Mr. Knapp's cattle raising proved to be embarrassing. He bought forty cows and thirty five bulls. The bulls kept everyone awake fighting for the females. After the first mating season he got rid of the cattle.

Mr. Knapp wanted to celebrate Christmas by sharing a huge fireworks display with his friends and neighbors. Folks lined the sound to see the fireworks. But it scared all the ducks away and they didn't come back for 4 or 5 years. He didn't do that again either.

A four hole golf course that could be played to 9 holes was in the cleared field.

Mr. Knapp had a barge that would ferry children and neighbors over to Currituck for special occasions such as May Day celebrations. My mother, Every Vance Williams Jones told me of these outings. The children were given gifts of clothing, shoes and other necessities at Christmas. Mother said those gifts were the only gifts she got for Christmas. Gifts from the Knapp Foundation are still being given today but only small remembrance gifts.

Joseph Palmer Knapp's hunting retreat on Mackay Island

Mr. Knapp built the school at Knotts Island and at Currituck and built the houses for the teachers to live in. Even a home economics teacher and music teacher were brought here. He paid all their salaries. He raised the vegetables for the lunches and furnished the meat and milk. You can see why so many of the older people of the Island praise his name. Many of the Islanders were able to keep their homes because Mr. Knapp paid their mortgage payments when they couldn't. He was a very generous man to his friends and neighbors. He lived on the island for thirty-two years.

In 1923 he began to develop the modern rural school system. He gave $50,000 a year to support the school system. He sent for the best teachers available from all over the world. He established free textbooks and free lunches. A nurse, doctor and dentist were hired to take care of the children. This was the first public school nurse in North Carolina in 1924. He used his boats and chauffeurs to transport the sick to the doctor. He was instrumental in establishing the Albemarle Hospital. He established Mutual Exchange, a credit exchange so farmers could buy their crops at wholesale prices and hold them until they could get the best price for them. Mr. Knapp died at 86 years old in January 1951 and is buried at the Moyock Hollywood Cemetery.[7]

Frederick C. Havemeyer recalls the Currituck Shooting Club

The first shooting trip I ever made was to Currituck. It was obvious I should go there first, because both my father and grandfather had done most of their shooting at Currituck. I went down by train to Cape Charles, and in the cold, early dawn boarded the steamer for Norfolk. My fellow travelers were all sportsmen. Duffel bags and guns were piled high in the cabin, everyone was talking ducks and geese....

From Norfolk, I went by car to Virginia Beach and then along the dunes to Currituck. As we bowled along on the sand, I wished I had been able to go down with a Currituck hunts-man before the turn of the century. In those days you went by train to Munden's Point, then sailed down the sound....

Dinner at Currituck Club is always a feast. The table groans with Hunger Creek oysters, roasted Teal and red wine. You eat until you cannot swallow another morsel, then you stand with your back to the fire and take part in the talk of shooting, past and present....

There was the day I...saw five thousand geese in the air at one time. The sky was simply filled with them. I took colored photographs of this amazing sight and mailed the film to be developed. The film came back with a letter telling me to clean my camera lens. The dirty lens was responsible for those spots in the sky.

Spots! They weren't spots—they were those myriad geese. When the film was projected on a screen you could see the geese very distinctly.[8]

Margaret M. West et al., Petitioners, v. Earl F. Slick et al., Respondents, North Carolina Supreme Court, February 27, 1985

Respondents are individuals and joint ventures owning a tract of land known as the "Pine Island property" approximately four miles long and from three hundred yards to three-quarters of a mile wide running between the Atlantic Ocean on the east and Currituck Sound on the west and lying between Corolla to the north and the Currituck–Dare County line to the south....

Petitioners are nine individuals, some of whom are owners of real property on the Outer Banks of Currituck County. Some of the petitioners are residents of Corolla, some of Knotts Island, and some are residents of other areas of Currituck County north of respondents' property. Yet others are nonresidents of North Carolina.

The property in question consists of sand beach, dunes and marsh, and comprises about four of the eleven miles of the outer banks between the Currituck–Dare County line and the Village of Corolla. The property has always been and largely still is wild, open land.

Pursuant to a private easement respondents permit certain individuals to cross their property on a new paved road. Respondents however have, by the use of chain link gates, a guard house and conspicuous signs, prohibited vehicular traffic by the general public, including petitioners, from crossing the

Pine Island property. Because vehicular access to Corolla from the north is blocked by the Back Bay National Wildlife Refuge and from the east and west by the Atlantic Ocean and Currituck Sound respectively, respondents in effect are denying the petitioners and the public the only available vehicular access to and from Corolla and the northern reaches of the Currituck outer banks. The respondents have denied access contending that the ways and easements across their property are private.[9]

The Brothers from Ohio

Two of the most iconic figures associated with the Outer Banks could hardly have been more different from the locals—in their formal dress, in the work they did for a living, and certainly in their leisure-time activities.

The residents of Kitty Hawk and environs saw Wilbur and Orville Wright as eccentrics—as did everyone else who knew of their quest for heavier-than-air flight, considered a fringe pursuit in their day. But the locals also respected diligence, ingenuity, and toughness. The Wrights traveled halfway across the country during "vacations" from their bicycle business in Dayton, Ohio. Their principal rewards were hunger, a lack of indoor plumbing and other comforts, plagues of mosquitoes, and heavy storms that threatened to destroy their tent and later their flimsy buildings. Kitty Hawk residents and the lifesavers at the Kill Devil Hills station helped the Wrights in their experiments as time permitted. Mutual respect and a few lifelong friendships grew.

The Wrights visited six different years. In 1900, 1901, and 1902, they made glider flights from the Kill Devil Hills dunes. In 1903, they made history's first powered heavier-than-air flights. In 1908, shortly before they went public with their invention, they returned for the world's first two-person flights. They last came together in 1911, when they were back to flying gliders. Wilbur and Orville were two of the most famous men in the world by then.

The initial excerpt below is Wilbur Wright's first formal

communication on the subject of flight. His modesty belies his and Orville's engineering genius. The Wrights essentially solved the flight problem by the off-season following their 1902 Outer Banks trip; they had only to add an engine to their airframe. It thus took them a mere three and a half years of part-time labor to end a quest humans had been pursuing for centuries.

The second excerpt is the response to Wilbur's inquiry to the Kitty Hawk weather station regarding local wind conditions. William Tate was a fisherman, a county commissioner, a former postmaster, and a one-man chamber of commerce. That said, his claim of steady ten- to twenty-mile-per-hour winds—music to Wilbur's ears—was woefully inaccurate. In camp, the Wrights were continually frustrated by periods of dead calm punctuated by forty-mile-per-hour blows, neither of which suited their purposes.

On the other hand, the third excerpt testifies to the wisdom of Tate's advice about not visiting after October 15. Just beyond that date in 1903—and two months before their famous flights—the Wrights lived through the major storm Wilbur describes to his sister. The letter is a good representation of the humor, self-deprecation, and storytelling talent possessed by both of the brothers.

Orville composed the next two pieces on the day the Wrights made history. One, from his diary, immortalizes the first-flight witnesses—all local men—and in particular the camera work of lifesaver John T. Daniels, who supposedly took only one photo his entire life, albeit a noteworthy one. The other is Orville's telegram to Ohio. Milton Wright, a bishop in the United Brethren Church, likely welcomed the news of his sons' return for Christmas as much as he did the report of their successful flights.

The next piece, from the *Norfolk Virginian-Pilot*, is the

world's first news report of powered flight. Usually credited to Harry Moore and Keville Glennan, it is a model of comical inaccuracy from the first of its descending headlines to Orville's cry of "Eureka" in the final line. But in the writers' defense, they were tasked with describing an entirely new technology on the basis of sketchy information gathered long-distance. The four flights of December 17, 1903, ranged from 120 feet to 852 feet. They were straight-line flights over sand and probably never rose more than 10 feet off the ground. Wilbur was thirty-six at the time and Orville thirty-two. Wilbur was dead of natural causes less than nine years later.

In the following excerpt, historian David Stick fondly recalls his attendance as a seven-year-old at the silver anniversary of the flights—and especially the time he spent beside the famous aviatrix who was his traveling companion.

Orville lived until 1948, long enough to witness non-stop transatlantic flight and early jet propulsion, but also World War II aerial devastation. Late in life, he expressed mixed feelings about the tragic byproducts of his invention: "I once thought the aeroplane would end wars. I now wonder whether the aeroplane and the atomic bomb can do it. It seems that ambitious rulers will sacrifice the lives and property of all their people to gain a little personal fame."[1] The final excerpt is from the remarks of Lieutenant General Jimmy Doolittle at the golden-anniversary celebration at Wright Brothers National Memorial in 1953. Doolittle won the Medal of Honor for leading a daring bombing raid on Japan from the carrier USS *Hornet* in April 1942, a major morale boost for American forces early in World War II. The cautionary note he sounded at Kill Devil Hills suggests how much the first fifty years of flight had changed the world.

William J. Tate, the Wrights' first host on the Outer Banks, with his
family on the porch of their home, which also served as the Kitty
Hawk post office. Film negative was damaged during a flood.
Courtesy of Library of Congress Prints & Photographs Division

Wilbur Wright to the Smithsonian Institution

DAYTON, MAY 30, 1899

I believe that simple flight at least is possible to man and
that the experiments and investigations of a large number of
independent workers will result in the accumulation of information and knowledge and skill which will finally lead to accomplished flight.

...I am about to begin a systematic study of the subject in
preparation for practical work to which I expect to devote
what time I can spare from my regular business. I wish to ob-
tain such papers as the Smithsonian Institution has published

on this subject, and if possible a list of other works in print in the English language. I am an enthusiast, but not a crank in the sense that I have some pet theories as to the proper construction of a flying machine. I wish to avail myself of all that is already known and then if possible add my mite to help on the future worker who will attain final success.[2]

William Tate to Wilbur Wright

KITTY HAWK, AUGUST 18, 1900

You would find here nearly any type of ground you could wish; you could, for instance, get a stretch of sandy land 1 mile by five with a bare hill in center 80 feet high, not a tree or bush anywhere to break the evenness of the wind current. This in my opinion would be a fine place; our winds are always steady, generally from 10 to 20 miles velocity per hour.

…Would advise you to come any time from Sept. 15 to Oct. 15. Don't wait until Nov. The autumn generally gets a little rough by Nov.

If you decide to try your machine here & come I will take pleasure in doing all I can for your convenience & success & pleasure, & I assure you you will find a hospitable people when you come among us.[3]

Wilbur Wright to Katharine Wright

KILL DEVIL HILLS, OCTOBER 18, 1903

The second day opened with the gale still continuing with a steady drizzling rain. The wind veered from the northwest to the north during the morning and dropped to about 30 miles, but after dinner it began to back up again. We set to work "tooth and nail" (using a hammer instead of our teeth however) putting braces inside our new building. The climax came about 4 o'clock when the wind reached 75 miles an hour.

Suddenly a corner of our tar-paper roof gave way under the pressure and we saw that if the trouble were not stopped the whole roof would probably go. Orville put on my heavy overcoat, and grabbing the ladder sallied forth from the south end of the building. At first it appeared that he was going down to repair some of the rents in the Big Hill which was being badly torn to pieces, for he began by walking backwards about 50 feet. After a while I saw him come back past the side opening in our partially raised awning door....Thereupon I sallied out to help him and after a tussle with the wind found him at the north end ready to set up the ladder. He quickly mounted to the edge of the roof when the wind caught under his coat and folded it back over his head. As the hammer and nails were in his pocket and up over his head he was unable to get his hands on them or to pull his coattails down, so he was compelled to descend again. The next time he put the nails in his mouth and took the hammer in his hand and I followed him up the ladder hanging on to his coattails. He swatted around a good little while trying to get a few nails in, and I became almost impatient for I had only my common coat on and was getting well soaked. He explained afterward that the wind kept blowing the hammer around so that three licks out of four hit the roof or his fingers instead of the nail. Finally the job was done and we rushed for cover. He took off the overcoat and felt his other coat and found it nice and dry, but after half an hour or so, finding that he was feeling wetter and wetter, he began a second investigation and found the inside of his coat sopping wet, while the outside was nice and dry. He had forgotten when he first felt of his coat, that it, as well as the overcoat, were practically inside out while he was working on the roof. The wind and rain continued through the night, but we took the advice of the Oberlin coach, "Cheer up, boys, there is no hope." We went to bed, and both slept soundly....The storm continued through Saturday and Sunday, but by Monday it had reared up so much that it finally fell over on its back and lay quiet....

The "whopper flying machine" is coming on all right and will probably be done about Nov. 1st.[4]

The 1903 machine on the launching track, prior to a failed trial three days before the famous powered flights. Four men from the Kill Devil Hills Life-Saving Station helped move it from the shed, accompanied by two small boys and a dog.
Courtesy of Library of Congress Prints & Photographs Division

Orville Wright's diary, December 17, 1903

When we got up a wind of between 20 and 25 miles was blowing from the north. We got the machine out early and put out the signal for the men at the [lifesaving] station [at Kill Devil Hills]. Before we were quite ready, John T. Daniels, W. S. Dough, A. D. Etheridge, W. C. Brinkley of Manteo, and Johnny Moore of Nags Head arrived. After running the engine and propellers a few minutes to get them in working order, I got on the machine at 10:35 for the first trial.... On slipping the rope the machine started off increasing in speed to probably 7 or 8 miles [per hour]. The machine lifted from the truck just as it was entering on the fourth rail. Mr. Daniels took a picture just as it left the tracks. I found the control of the front rudder quite difficult on account of its being balanced too near the center and thus had a tendency to turn itself when started so that the rudder was turned too far on one side and then too far on the other. As a result the machine would rise suddenly to about 10 feet. And then as suddenly, on turning the rudder, dart for the ground. A sudden dart when out about 100 feet from the end of the tracks ended the flight. Time about 12 seconds.[5]

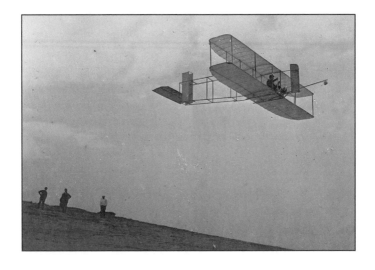

Orville Wright conducting gliding experiments
at Kill Devil Hills in 1911
Courtesy of Library of Congress Prints & Photographs Division

Telegram from Orville Wright to his father, December 17, 1903

Success four flights Thursday morning all against twenty-one mile wind started from level with engine power alone average speed through air thirty-one miles longest 57 seconds inform press home Christmas.[6]

Norfolk Virginian-Pilot article, December 18, 1903

FLYING MACHINE SOARS THREE MILES IN TEETH OF HIGH WIND OVER SAND HILLS AND WAVES ON CAROLINA COAST

NO BALLOON ATTACHED TO AID IT

THREE YEARS OF HARD, SECRET WORK BY TWO OHIO BROTHERS CROWNED WITH SUCCESS

ACCOMPLISHED WHAT LANGLEY FAILED AT

WITH MAN AS PASSENGER HUGE MACHINE FLIES UNDER PERFECT CONTROL

BOX KITE PRINCIPLE WITH TWO PROPELLERS

The problem of aerial navigation without the use of a balloon has been solved at last.

Over the sand hills of the North Carolina coast yesterday, near Kitty Hawk, two Ohio men proved that they could soar through the air in a flying machine of their own construction, with the power to steer it and speed it at will. This, too, in the face of a wind blowing at the confirmed velocity of twenty-one miles an hour.

Like a monster bird, the invention hovered above the breakers and circled over the rolling sand hills at the command of its navigator and, after soaring for three miles, it gracefully descended to earth again and rested lightly upon the spot selected by the man in the car as a suitable landing place.

While the United States government has been spending thousands of dollars in an effort to make practicable the ideas of Professor [Samuel] Langley of the Smithsonian Institute [*sic*], Wilbur and Orville Wright, two brothers, natives of Dayton, O., have quietly, even secretly, perfected their invention, and put it to a successful test.

They are not yet ready that the world should know the methods they have adopted in conquering the air, but the *Virginian-Pilot* is able to state authentically the nature of their invention, its principle and its chief dimensions.

HOW THE MACHINE WAS BUILT

The idea of the box kite has been adhered to strictly in the basic formation of the flying machine.

A huge framework of light timbers, 33 feet wide, five feet deep and five feet across the top forms the machine proper.

This is covered with a tough, but light canvas.

In the center, and suspended just below the bottom plane is the small gasoline engine which furnishes the motive power for the propelling and elevating wheels.

There are two six-bladed propellers, one arranged just below the center of the frame, so gauged as to exert an upward force when in motion, and the other extends horizontally to the rear from the center of the car, furnishing the forward impetus.

Protruding from the center of the car is a huge fan-shaped rudder of canvas, stretched upon a frame of wood. This rudder is controlled by the navigator and may be moved to each side, raised or lowered.

START WITH SUCCESS

Wilbur Wright, the chief inventor of the machine, sat in the operator's car and when all was ready his brother unfastened the catch which held the invention at the top of the slope.

The big box began to move slowly at first, acquiring velocity as it went, and when half way down the hundred feet the engine was started.

The propeller in the rear immediately began to revolve at a high rate of speed, and when the end of the incline was reached the machine shot out into space without a perceptible fall.

By this time the elevating propeller was also in motion, and, keeping its altitude, the machine slowly began to go higher and higher until it finally soared sixty feet above the ground.

Maintaining this height by the action of the under wheel, the navigator increased the revolutions of the rear propeller, and the forward speed of the huge affair increased until a velocity of eight miles an hour was attained.

All this time the machine headed into a twenty-one mile wind.

COAST FOLK AMAZED

The little crowd of fisher folk and coast guards, who have been watching the construction of the machine with unconcerned curiosity since September 1st, were amazed.

They endeavored to race over the sand and keep up with the thing of the air, but it soon distanced them and continued its flight alone, save the man in the car.

Steadily it pursued its way, first tacking to port, then to starboard, and then driving straight ahead.

"It is a success," declared Orville Wright to the crowd on the beach after the first mile had been covered.

But the inventor waited. Not until he had accomplished three miles, putting the machine through all sorts of maneuvers en route, was he satisfied.

Then he selected a suitable place to land, and, gracefully circling, drew his invention slowly to the earth, where it settled, like some big bird, in the chosen spot.

"Eureka," he cried, as did the alchemist of old.[7]

David Stick recalls the twenty-fifth anniversary

The day was the 17th of December, 1928, the 25th anniversary of the Wright Brothers' first flights in a heavier than air machine at the base of nearby Kill Devil Hill. A big celebration was planned, beginning with ceremonies at Kill Devil Hill in which Orville Wright located the site of the original flight so a permanent marker could be placed there. This was followed by a banquet and speeches in the pavilion at Virginia Dare Shores. In addition to Orville Wright, a number of other aviation dignitaries were there, intermingled with local, State and national politicians. It was a gala event....

...I still have a set of four prized pictures, two of them showing the masses of people and parked cars along the bay shore, with the Virginia Dare Shores buildings in the background; and the other two, taken from a boat, showing the mobs on the dock and entering the pavilion. But I have, in addition, one very prized personal memory; for on that day, less than a week before my eighth birthday, I rode from Virginia Dare Shores to Kill Devil Hill—and back again—in the rear of an old pickup truck with Amelia Earhart, the famous aviatrix, who held me close to keep me from falling off the bouncing vehicle.[8]

Lieutenant General Jimmy Doolittle's remarks at the golden anniversary, December 17, 1953

Celebrations honoring the Wright brothers are being held in communities all over the United States. Word is being spread by press, radio, and television. Many foreign nations are marking the anniversary. It is ironical that the 50th anniversary of powered flight has received considerably more attention than was originally paid to the flight it celebrates....

The real meaning of the Wrights' first flight and the significance of this anniversary are not in the events themselves but in what they lead to—in what follows them. There was no immediate practical value in flying 120 feet. But there was immeasurable value in knowing how to do it, in proving, for the first time, that it could be done and in learning how to fly easier, better—farther and faster....

When the Wrights had finished their work in 1903 and had packed up their improbable-looking plane and closed camp to go back to Ohio, the air was no more buoyant than before, and the Atlantic was just as wide as ever. Yet because of the Wrights' work, the oceans have shrunk—in time—and the continents have been joined through the air. The wide places of the earth—the seas, the Arctic wastes, and the skies above them—that once stood as bulwarks against attack are now broad avenues of approach. They no longer protect us. Instead, they must be watched and defended.[9]

The 1952 flyover during the forty-ninth anniversary
of the Wright brothers' powered flights
Courtesy of State Archives of North Carolina

The National Seashores

The United States has only ten national seashores, and two of them are on the Outer Banks. And depending on the width of Ocracoke Inlet on any given day, they come within a mile of touching.

Understanding where the seashores begin and end—and stop and continue—is challenging, given the local geography and the profusion of wildlife refuges, nature preserves, and national and state parks and memorials on the Banks and the immediate mainland coast.

Cape Hatteras National Seashore—America's first seashore park—is the most-visited attraction on the Outer Banks. It is part of a National Park Service administrative grouping that includes Wright Brothers National Memorial and Fort Raleigh National Historic Site. The seashore stretches seventy miles beginning at Whalebone Junction south of Nags Head. It extends south to where Bodie Island ends at Oregon Inlet, claiming the Bodie Island Lighthouse and a beach-bound shipwreck, the *Laura A. Barnes*, en route. Then, across Oregon Inlet, it omits the northern portion of Hatteras Island (administered by the United States Fish and Wildlife Service as Pea Island National Wildlife Refuge) and picks up again at Rodanthe, from which it extends to the end of Hatteras Island, claiming the Cape Hatteras Lighthouse but omitting the several small communities down to Hatteras Village. Across Hatteras Inlet, it encompasses all of Ocracoke Island except for the village, though it curls around its western portion to pick up the Ocracoke Light

Station. Driving access to the northern end of the seashore is via the bridges at Kitty Hawk and from Roanoke Island. Ferry access at the southern end is from Swan Quarter and Cedar Island to Ocracoke. A shorter ferry ride provides the only transit between Hatteras and Ocracoke Islands.

Because of its remoteness and difficulty of access, Cape Lookout National Seashore is the third-least-visited of America's seashore parks (ahead of only Fire Island in New York and Cumberland Island in Georgia). It stretches fifty-six miles, beginning in the north at Portsmouth Island, located across Ocracoke Inlet from Ocracoke Island; Portsmouth is not under most conditions a distinct landmass and is considered part of North Core Banks, rather than a separate island. The seashore extends southward through South Core Banks to Cape Lookout, encompassing the Cape Lookout Lighthouse. Across Barden Inlet, it includes Shackleford Banks, which runs east-west, almost perpendicular to the rest of the park. The seashore also includes part of the inshore Harkers Island, the site of its administrative offices. Access is entirely by ferry—from Ocracoke, Harkers Island, and the mainland towns of Beaufort, Davis, and Atlantic—to various portions of the seashore. Rather than skirting existing towns as does Cape Hatteras National Seashore, Cape Lookout includes the pristine ghost village of Portsmouth and the site of the late, great Diamond City, once a village of five hundred at the eastern end of Shackleford Banks.

Robert Vogel, former superintendent at Cape Lookout, expressed reverence for the residents of bygone days: "America's national parks were places of human feeling before they became parks. They are ancestral homelands. People lived and died there. They shared emotional, spiritual, intellectual, and sensual perceptions about the land—its sounds, smell, and feel; its skies, wildlife, plants, and water. We are coming to understand that parks become richer when we see them through the eyes of people whose ancestors once lived there."[1] The first two excerpts below partake of that sentiment. In one, Joel Hancock shares memories of his legendary Diamond City forbear. In the other, Tony Seamon Jr. talks about the endurance of Portsmouth Village.

The third excerpt is a piece from the *Elizabeth City Independent* that is often credited with launching the national seashore movement. Frank Stick, the father of historian David Stick, was an illustrator, editorialist, real-estate developer, architectural designer, and conservationist whose influence on the Outer Banks is still felt half a century after his death. Stick ends his Depression-era missive with a direct appeal to the man most capable of making his dream come true.

It was just over four years from the publication of Stick's July 1933 article to the creation of Cape Hatteras National Seashore. The next excerpt is a portion of the founding legislation.

Nature-based recreation—hiking, windsurfing, kayaking, fishing, shell collecting—is central at the seashores. But the wildlife are the stars. Bird watching is popular. The wild-horse herd on Shackleford Banks is widely known. And last but certainly not least are the sea turtles. Dr. Matthew Godfrey is a sea turtle biologist with the North Carolina Wildlife Resources Commission whose territory includes Cape Lookout. The fifth excerpt, from Godfrey's blog for the North Carolina Sea Turtle Project, suggests his range of duties and the measure of devotion the turtles inspire in both professionals and volunteers.

Unfortunately, where fragile wildlife must coexist with human habitation, conflicts result. The final three excerpts concern the ongoing controversy at Cape Hatteras. The first two are from the website of Congressman Walter B. Jones Jr., Republican representative from North Carolina's Third Congressional

District since 1995. In those excerpts, "visitor access" is code for "beach driving." It is illustrative of the complexities of his job that, whereas Jones here comes down solidly on the side of free access at the possible expense of wildlife, he has also been instrumental in protecting the Shackleford horses.

The final piece is by ardent conservationist Ted Williams, who details how heated matters can get at an outwardly peaceful seashore.

Joel Hancock recalls his great-grandfather, a Diamond City legend

Billy [Hancock] died in 1914…but he was such a large character that stories were told about him a lot.…Billy was famous for several things; one is speed that's probably the most well depicted one.

According to the legend…he knocked the last leg out of the old lighthouse [the 1812 Cape Lookout Lighthouse] that was torn down about 1858 to be replaced by the lighthouse there. It was because he could run so fast they thought that he could clear himself of whatever debris that might be falling otherwise. You ask yourself, why didn't they do it some other way? But none-the-less…he tripped in trying to escape and so they didn't know how fast he could run, but he could crawl 25 mph!

There was a certain slyness as well as speed.…He would nest himself to the windward side to a flock of ducks and then when he startled them they would try to fly off but they always flew into the wind which would be into him. So he would always catch a duck anytime that he would like.[2]

Tony Seamon Jr. explains the survival of Portsmouth Village, uninhabited since 1971

The problem we're having right now [is] wind insurance.…And, it's kind of funny. Look at Portsmouth Island.

And look how that church is there and the other old places that's there and you know they've gone through more hell. They don't have any steel cables, no pilings, nothing. They're just sitting on top of the ground, that's it.... They must have done something right. It's the material they had. I always heard a boat builder can build a house, but a carpenter can't build a boat.... And I've said it's bred into them, just like the people that built over on the Banks. Just like the houses that were in Diamond City and all. They survived because it was in their bones and they had the building materials to use it. Now we don't and everybody is paying for it. Anybody should get a discount, it's those houses...that are still there that have been in a natural wind tunnel all those years.[3]

Aerial view of Portsmouth Island
Courtesy of National Park Service, Cape Hatteras National Seashore

Frank Stick article that inspired a movement

Within a single generation, with commendable foresight, our legislators have created and made accessible to the public, a national park system which embraces thousands of square miles of forests, mountains, lakes and desert....

Yet no moneys ever expended by Congressional edict and through presidential approval have ever advantaged the public more....No matter how divided they may have been upon economic and purely political issues, they have been single minded upon the one proposition that the success and the prosperity of a nation is not dependent wholly upon ponderable and physical things; but that the opportunity for healthful outdoor recreation, and communion with nature is as indispensable to national progression, as are commercial enterprises, educational and political discipline, or any of the manifold labors and endeavors of a modern civilization....

Most of these parks and reservations are located in the extreme west, and are therefore in general use by but a small percentage of the American people, yet within the past few years have been consumated [*sic*] several notable projects in the east, including the Great Smoky Mountain [*sic*] National Park....Yet it has seemed to me a strange and unfathomable thing that no sustained and general effort has ever been made to reserve for public use any considerable tract or body of land, of that character and type which is universally conceded to be the most attractive and interesting to the vacationist, and which, from a standpoint of health giving and environmental advantages; inspirational appeal and day after day livableness, offers more to the general public than can the most inspiring stretch of mountains, the most impressive forests or the clearest of lakes and streams. I speak now of our seashore....

...There still exists, what I believe to be the most attractive, unique and enchanting coastal section in America, and one which can be acquired through condemnation proceedings and, through state and private gift, at a cost per mile of less than would be charged for a hundred foot lot on our northern coast. A tract twenty-five miles in length, bounded by the ocean on one side, and by Pamlico Sound on the other, could be taken over for less than the price of five miles of concrete highway....

From a standpoint of climate…this section I have in mind could scarce be improved upon. Such high extremes of temperature as occur even at famous northern resorts, are unknown, yet, because of its close proximity to the Gulf Stream, the winter climate varies little from that of Jacksonville, Florida. Tornadoes have never visited this region, and high winds are a rarity.…For the seeker for rest and the opportunity to relax body and soul under the ennobling spell of the sea, or in the peaceful solitude of sun-kissed sounds, I do not know where could be found a territory comparable to it.…

…Cape Hatteras holds a fearsome sound to some. Many have thought of it as a storm swept, wind beaten and barren coast, yet nothing could further escape the facts.…Unfortunately, some few of the good people who dwell in the scattered villages of this section, have helped to stimulate the false impression that exists. Some there are who prefer to consider themselves as a hardy though suffering folk, braving inclemencies of weather, and privation. A hardy folk they are, and worthy. They could scarce know a section where life is simpler and less exciting; where the days flow more smoothly through their accustomed grooves, and where the people have to a less degree to contend against the worries and the complexities of our present civilization.…

We have in this country a certain citizen who knows the overpowering charm and allure of the rushing, ever changing tide; who knows the feel of salt spray in his face and the smell of the salty breeze to his nostrils.…This man I speak of is an outstanding citizen of this generation, and one whose name will go down in history, I think as the savior of a nation sore distressed.…Some time, certainly, a loving and appreciative nation will create a memorial to perpetuate in a material way, the name of this great and good citizen of these United States. Lying within the borders of that territory where American civilization saw its birth…what more fitting then, than that this mighty coastal park, with all its potentialities for happiness, for health and for mental, moral and physical uplift, be dedicated to Franklin D. Roosevelt?[4]

"An Act to provide for the establishment of the Cape Hatteras National Seashore," August 17, 1937

Be it enacted by the Senate and House of Representatives of the United States of America in Congress assembled, That when title to all the lands except those within the limits of established villages…within the area of approximately one hundred square miles on the islands of Chicamacomico, Ocracoke, Bodie, Roanoke, and Collington [*sic*], and the waters and the lands beneath the waters adjacent thereto shall have been vested in the United States, said area shall be, and is hereby, established, dedicated, and set apart as a national seashore for the benefit and enjoyment of the people and shall be known as the Cape Hatteras National Seashore….

Sec. 4. Except for certain portions of the area, deemed to be especially adaptable for recreational uses, particularly swimming, boating, sailing, fishing, and other recreational activities of similar nature…the said area shall be permanently reserved as a primitive wilderness and no development…for the convenience of visitors shall be undertaken which would be incompatible with the preservation of the unique flora and fauna or the physiographic conditions now prevailing in this area.[5]

Excerpts from the blog of Dr. Matthew Godfrey, sea turtle biologist

MARCH 2, 2003

Here at the northern limit of the nesting range of loggerheads in the West Atlantic, winter is slowly coming to an end.

Increasing water and sand temperatures mean that soon nesting females will be coming back to lay their eggs on our sandy beaches. Although I enjoy all aspects of working with sea turtles, there is nothing quite like the sight of a tiny hatchling scrambling from its nest to the ocean, except perhaps a whole group of hatchlings marching together towards the surf.

JUNE 5, 2003

In North America, tis the season for turtle migration. That includes not only sea turtles, but also land and freshwater turtles. Cars are a major source of mortality for land and freshwater turtles at this time of year, as they attempt to cross roads. Whenever I see a turtle crossing a road, I always stop my car on the shoulder and try to get the turtle to the other side before it is hit. Unfortunately, many times the turtles are crushed before I can get to them, and sometimes I nearly get hit myself. There is no easy solution, except to slow down and keep your eyes peeled for walking shells that are trying to cross the road; when you see one, give it lots of space.

AUGUST 21, 2003

…Adult Kemp's ridley turtles are a rarity in North Carolina. So it was with some surprise that in June 2003 a nesting female Kemp's ridley was discovered nesting on the beach near Cape Lookout in North Carolina. The turtle was laying its eggs in the middle of the day, a normal behavior for this species. The nest emerged recently and the nest inventory revealed that 73 out of 80 eggs total produced hatchlings. Two live turtles were still in the nest and were released to scramble to the ocean.

AUGUST 26, 2003

Sometimes, people say the most interesting things.…
A few weeks ago, [colleagues] Wendy, Larisa and I were

lucky enough to conduct a necropsy on a dead loggerhead turtle with some schoolkids who wanted to learn more about coastal marine ecology. They were all motivated enough to put up with the pungent odors produced by our specimen, which was already impressive. The questions they asked and the ideas they expressed were quite remarkable. My favorite statement of the day came from one of the kids who was talking about the different species of sea turtles. I asked him to name them all, and he had trouble recalling leatherbacks. I tried prompting him by saying that the forgotten species looked a bit different than the other ones. "Oh, now I remember!" he cried. "Leatherbacks! They look like watermelons."

Sea turtles crawl to sea after hatching release in 2012.
National Park Service, Cape Hatteras National Seashore

SEPTEMBER 20, 2003

Hurricane Isabelle came and went. It was not so bad in the center of the North Carolina coast. To the south it was less brutal, but the Outer Banks in the northern half of the state were hit hard and heavy. Fortunately most of the nests laid in the 2003 season had already emerged by the time Isabelle arrived, but high tides, large swashes and eroding tides have threatened the majority of the remaining nests. Few dead or injured turtles have been reported, although I did get a call about a lethargic loggerhead found in the water just down the street from my house. The volunteers, who monitor the beaches, take care of the nests and watch for strandings, are cleaning up the mess and trying to get back on schedule.

FEBRUARY 8, 2004

Many sea turtle projects rely heavily on volunteers to get the work done. The North Carolina Sea Turtle Project is no different. There are over 500 participants who contribute their time to monitoring nests and responding to strandings. Most of these participants are volunteers. I am always amazed at how willing and dedicated these people are. This is particularly true when it comes to our requests to collect samples from dead turtles. Yet, so many people have come forward and offered to retrieve flippers, eyeballs and other parts from sometimes rotting carcasses. The good will and enthusiasm of our sea turtle volunteers was evident at a recent training workshop we held in Corolla, North Carolina. More than a dozen people braved the cool breezy garage of the local fire station to learn how to remove the humerus bone and also to classify sex of a dead turtle that they might find on the beach in their area.

AUGUST 11, 2004

End of the summer in North Carolina means the start of hatching season. Despite the low numbers of nests laid this year and the recent hurricane [Alex, which hit on August 3], there is still the opportunity to see some live hatchlings on the beach. The nests are usually excavated in the early evening, some 72 hours after signs of first emergence by hatchlings from the nest. In this case, two of the sea turtle project participants started digging up the nest with less than 20 observers on hand. This number swelled to 50 or more, as more people were attracted by the crowd on the beach. Three live loggerheads were found at the bottom of the nest and allowed to crawl to the ocean, much to the delight of the onlookers. One little girl asked me if it was my job to work with turtles. When I said yes, she said, "That is what I want to be when I get older: a sea turtle worker." Clearly, these kinds of experiences do have an impact on people who participate.[6]

"Where I Stand," by Congressman Walter B. Jones Jr.

I believe we must balance the needs of a healthy environment with the needs of a vibrant economy. In recent years, the federal government has in too many instances veered away from common-sense environmental protection and instead pursued an ideological agenda. These policies destroy jobs and do little, if anything, to help the people, wildlife or plants they purport to protect.

In Eastern North Carolina, we have seen these short-sighted policies on many levels. Some examples are the excessive restrictions on visitor access at Cape Hatteras National Seashore, a laundry list of unnecessary fishing regulations, and regulatory vetoes of essential infrastructure projects such as jetties at Oregon Inlet and replacement of Bonner Bridge.[7]

"House Again Passes Jones' Bill to Restore Cape Hatteras Beach Access," February 2014

Today, the House of Representatives voted to approve Congressman Walter B. Jones' (NC-3) proposal to repeal excessive restrictions on human access to Cape Hatteras National Seashore Recreational Area.…[The proposed strategy is] supported by a 113-page Biological Opinion issued by the U.S. Fish and Wildlife Service, which found that it would not jeopardize piping plover, sea turtles, or other species of concern.

"The last thing we need in Eastern North Carolina is unnecessary government regulation stifling job creation and economic growth," said Congressman Jones. "I am grateful to my colleagues in the House for voting to approve this common-sense measure, which strikes the appropriate balance between protecting the species that live in the Cape Hatteras area and protecting the taxpayers' right to access the recreational areas that they own. Now it is time for the Senate to act."[8]

Aerial view of Cape Point near Buxton

Conservation writer Ted Williams on the beach-driving controversy

As summer winds down, a war is heating up on the Outer Banks of North Carolina [at] America's oldest national seashore. On one side are property-rights types who drive off-road vehicles, or ORVs, and until recently could do practically anything they pleased on the state's 67 miles of beach. On the other side are wildlife advocates and government agencies, who are trying to rein them in.

For 30 years I've birded and fished on these barrier beaches that seal the coast of North Carolina and Pamlico Sound from the rages of the Atlantic Ocean....

Wildlife advocates on the Outer Banks will no longer speak to me on the record because they fear for their lives. They've had nails thrown in their driveways. They've been ejected from restaurants and shops. They've been told to look under their cars before turning on the ignition....

...Wildlife advocates, too, have had directions to their houses posted on the Internet. Their photos and names have been printed on "wanted" posters, worn on T-shirts and hung in public places. A typical poster reads, "Wanted for the economic ruin of Hatteras Island. The man is one of the leaders of the beach ban. Consider him dangerous to your livelihoods and recreation."

Actually, the local economy is booming, in no small measure because pedestrians, who outnumber ORV operators 90 to 1, suddenly feel safe on the beach....

On ORV websites, the push for new regulations has elicited fits of invective. One negotiator representing wildlife interests was called an "econazi" and a "self-centered, left wing idiot... an insult to every piece of excrement out there....Once we retake Congress, public enemies such as himself and the idiots we elected who have supported him will only have survival to fear."

Another post reads: "As for the birds, to hell with 'em."...

One of my duties as conservation editor for *Fly Rod & Reel* magazine is administering a fishing/conservation blog where I report extensively on ORV damage to Outer Banks wildlife. While residents accuse us of attempting "to drive man from Hatteras Island,"...we hear from ethical anglers who are merely outshouted—not outnumbered—by the motorheads.

A commenter who goes by "Redfish," writes: "Cape Hatteras National Seashore is a better place because [of the regulations]....The absurd bill [Congressman] Jones sponsored threatens this seashore and every other seashore."

Redfish is referring to "The Beach Roadkill Bill," as it is called by its critics, that has passed the House and is now before the Senate where it's being ballyhooed by North Carolina senators Richard Burr (R) and Kay Hagan (D). It would do away with the ORV regulations.

The regulations have made a huge difference. This year's nesting statistics for birds are not yet available. But in the 2007 breeding season—the last before the regulations—there were 212 colonial-waterbird nests on the seashore; in 2011 there were 1,150....

During the same period, black skimmer nests increased from 0 to 99; least tern nests from 194 to 1,048; gull-billed tern nests from 0 to 15; common tern nests from 18 to 112; fledged oystercatcher chicks from 10 to 24. In 2007 there were 82 sea-turtle nests; so far in 2012 there have been 217—a record.

If Congress nixes the ORV regulations, major destruction of wildlife—including endangered species—will resume. National seashores belong to all Americans, not just a few loud, local property-rights radicals who have bullied their way to dominance.[9]

World War II

Following the Japanese attack on Pearl Harbor on December 7, 1941, and Germany's war declaration four days later, the United States had to increase military production, officials had to humble themselves and take advice from allies, and Americans had to embrace a wartime mentality.

The lag time in all three areas brought devastating results along the Outer Banks, littering the shores and illuminating the nighttime skies. Running the U-boat gauntlet of Germany's Operation Drumbeat, the brave souls of the Merchant Marine were protected—when they were protected at all—by inadequate arms and a haphazard collection of craft designed for other purposes. Great Britain, which had experience in the matter, recommended coastal convoys navigating a zigzag pattern, yet vessels continued to run the Gulf Stream solo and straight ahead. Some coastal residents resisted blackout measures, unwittingly backlighting merchant vessels for the benefit of U-boats hunting at night.

Though only five U-boats were initially dispatched across the Atlantic to the American coast, the pickings proved so easy that a total of sixty-five ultimately participated in the first seven months of 1942. In that span, they sank just under four hundred ships, killing nearly five thousand people. The Outer Banks, particularly the Cape Hatteras vicinity, saw the heaviest concentration of destruction. Explosions shattered windows. Bodies, oil, and debris floated ashore.

The stakes could not have been higher. Great Britain, which

had borne the heaviest burden of the war, was in danger of falling. It was dependent on merchant vessels for all its fuel and half its food. Atlantic shipping was its lifeline.

The speed with which America turned the coastal war is a testament to the nation's industrial capacity, innovation, and public spirit in those times. Sonar arrays, reconnaissance planes, and blimps scouted out U-boats, and destroyers and torpedo bombers hunted them. Meanwhile, merchant ships began running in convoys and residents installed black curtains on their homes and businesses and covered the upper halves of their automobile headlights. By late July 1942, Germany discontinued its U-boat efforts off the United States. It was a stunning turnaround, capping a brief but momentous period in Outer Banks history.

The first excerpt below is from Nell Wise Wechter's beloved *Taffy of Torpedo Junction*, a young-adult novel set at the height of the coastal war. With Taffy, pony Sailor and boxer Brandy, Outer Banks–brogue–talking Gramp, and noble but slow-thinking Big Jens on the case, the fate of Hitler's minions was a foregone conclusion.

The next piece is an account from the MS *City of New York*, torpedoed east of Cape Hatteras by Oberleutnant Georg Lassen of the U-160 in March 1942. Alviro Santiago's rescue of a young boy, it turned out, was no better than the third most incredible story to come from his ship's demise. A Yugoslavian woman gave birth under dreadful conditions aboard another lifeboat; her "lifeboat baby" became a headline for a nation starved for good news. Yet another lifeboat drifted all the way to the New Jersey coast before being recovered fourteen days after the sinking; only thirteen of its original twenty occupants were alive.

The third piece, from L. Van Loan Naisawald's *In Some Foreign Field*, treats the U-558's sinking of the HMS *Bedfordshire* off Ocracoke in May 1942. The *Bedfordshire* was on loan from the Royal Navy as part of a fleet of twenty-four former fishing trawlers converted for use on anti-submarine patrols. None of its crew survived.

The fourth excerpt is a newspaper account of the loss of two men of the Civil Air Patrol and their plane while on anti-submarine patrol duty. Ironically, the crash took place in December 1942, after U-boats had departed the coast. The site, New Inlet, has passed into and out of existence before and since World War II.

The following piece is the schedule of the dedication ceremony at Ocracoke's British Cemetery, site of the graves of four men of the *Befordshire*—Sub-Lieutenant Thomas Cunningham, telegraphist Stanley Craig, and two unidentified sailors. On that small piece of British soil on an American island, a memorial service is held yearly around May 11, the date of the sinking.

The next two pieces are accounts by Outer Banks residents.

Gordon Willis tells of a surprise encounter with a U-boat in which luck was on the side of the locals. The wartime air was thick with rumors, the most persistent of which was the unfounded claim that German spies—"sabbatiers," as Willis puts it—were landing on the Outer Banks. Willis and his interviewer also touch on another rumor in discussing the Germans' machine-gunning of survivors in lifeboats. It is far more likely that those empty boats were shot up by American vessels or planes trying to sink them so future rescue efforts wouldn't waste time tracking them.

Jakie Robertson's brief account tells of the day during the war when Portsmouth Island was mistakenly bombed.

In the eighth excerpt, O. Lawrence Burnette Jr. describes his immediate postwar adventures at the blimp base near Elizabeth City, on the mainland west of the Corolla-Duck area.

In the final excerpt, Reinhard Hardegen, former captain of the U-123, tells of meeting a survivor from one of the ships he had torpedoed fifty years earlier. Originally a pilot, Hardegen was transferred to submarine service after a crash left him with a shortened leg. Under his command, the U-123 sank twenty-two ships. A survivor himself of one of the most hazardous war duties imaginable, Hardegen was still alive, age 101, as of this writing.

Taffy and Gramp parse the U-boat menace; Hitler put on notice

Taffy had just fed Sailor his evening oats and carried in an armful of driftwood that evening in January [1942]. Gramp was trimming the wick in the oil lamp. Just as Taffy threw down the wood, three deafening explosions boomed across the water; and then three more. The little shack rocked; the windows rattled. Taffy's eardrums felt blasted.

They quickly opened the door and went outside. Up the beach, off Rodanthe or Gull Shoal—somewhere in that vicinity—two tremendous fires were blazing over the ocean. They seemed to be about ten miles offshore. Another explosion smote their ears, sending up a bigger blaze near the first two.

"How awful!" Taffy shuddered clutching her grandfather's hand.

"Subs hittin' a convoy," Gramp told her. "Tankers loaded with oil. That's what it is."

"But sinking three ships at a time," Taffy whimpered. "It's horrible!"

"Yes, child," Gramp tried to comfort her, "war always is. But think of them little children over in Europe, and all the sufferin' in the Pacific oislands."

"But the subs come so close to shore, Gramp. Isn't there anything our ships can do to protect themselves?"

They walked back to the shack. "It's a bad toime, roight now," Gramp told her. "The truth of the matter is, we was caught in an awful state of unpreparedness, what with them Japs bummin' us at Pearl Harbor and us a-troyin' to help the British keep the sea lanes open 'twixt here and Europe. It'll take toime, but don't you fret. Our country won't take all this loyin' down. You mark moy words."[1]

Bellboy Alviro Santiago turns hero upon the sinking of the *City of New York*

On [March] 29th, [1942,] the day before our arrival at New York I got up at 0600 and after breakfast I went up to the dining room to attend to my routine work. At 1145 I went to my cabin to call my partner Joachin Rodriguez for his 1200–1600 watch. I noticed that he had a fever and wasn't feeling good so I told the Chief Steward I would do his work. I then went to do my rounds on the Promenade Deck.

There I met the deck steward Arthur Comone, a good friend of mine. He said he was going to his cabin for aspirin as he had a terrible headache. I told him I would take care of the afternoon tea for him.

At 1545, when I was making the last round with the tea, there was a terrific explosion. I found myself in the air and then I landed on my back. When I tried to get up I found that my left leg was badly broken and I was bleeding through my nose, mouth and ears. I was in terrible pain.

At that moment I saw a little boy about 5 yrs old crying hysterically, and calling his Mommy. I called him and he came running to me. We both fell down. But I struggled to my feet and put a child's life jacket on him. I looked around and there was considerable confusion and panic. I saw three lifeboats being launched.

I struggled to the rail holding the boy in my arms. I called to the men in the boat to come and get the boy. They told me to jump with him into the water and to do it fast as the ship was going down rapidly.

Then came the second explosion. The concussion blew me into the water holding the boy. I never let go of him. One of the boats came along and picked us up.

There were three other lifeboats in the water with passengers and crew. In my boat there were forty-five people, passengers and crew. Later on I found the boy's mother was in our boat.

We were in the boat until midnight of the following day when we were picked up by the USS *Roper*. I was rushed to the ship's hospital where the doctor found my leg broken in three places, my hip dislocated, and my back was badly injured. I was in much pain and was given a shot of morphine. Around 0500 we arrived at the Norfolk Naval Base. Before they put me ashore, the passengers and Navy crew came to shake hands with me and wish me luck. I asked the Navy officer why everyone was shaking my hand? He told me for saving the life of the boy. I told him anyone would do the same. He replied, "Not in the condition you are in, son!"

I was taken to the Naval Hospital in Norfolk along with other wounded seamen. I was there for 3 weeks in a cast. I was then moved to the Marine Hospital in Staten Island, NY via a ferry, ambulance, and train. I was there a month and sent home to be treated at the clinic at Hudson & Jay Street. After being treated there for 3 months, I was sent to the Kermit Roosevelt estate in Oyster Bay, Long Island for convalescence. After two months there I was given a "fit for duty" slip. After resting at home for 2 weeks I registered at the union hall. I was still limping a little bit. On October 23, 1942 I signed on the troopship SS *John Ericsson*. I stayed on her through the invasions of Sicily, New Guinea, and the Normandy beaches.

My two friends, whom I mentioned previously, Joachin

Rodriguez and Arthur Comone went down with the ship and were among the crew members of the MS *City of New York* who were lost.[2]

The U-558 sinks the HMS *Bedfordshire*

Gunther Krech became something of a legend in the German submarine service, for he carried with him a seagoing aquarium. In this tank were pet fish whom he had named after crowned heads and prime ministers of the powers at war with Germany. [Dutch queen] Wilhelmina was a handsome goldfish; she met an unfortunate end when she fell from a spoon into the bilges while the aquarium was being cleaned. Churchill was a small temperamental pirate fish. He had made three patrols before he succumbed and was ceremoniously interred in an alcohol-filled glass tube, which was then suspended from the lamp in the wardroom....

... At 10:07 P.M. [on May 11, 1942], a ship's silhouette appeared off the sub's stern. A quick second look showed it was apparently a patrol vessel. Kapitanleutnant Krech, his mind probably keenly aware that he had no sinkings to show for his month at sea, promptly turned to attack the unsuspecting ship, using a surface attack—the preferred German sub tactic at this stage of the war.

Krech maneuvered his sub into a firing position. Through his attack periscope, he tracked the trawler. She was moving at about six knots and at a range of 1000 meters. The target data went to the fire direction plotters, and a torpedo course was established. At 11:26 P.M. Gunther Krech barked: Fire one! Fire two! With that he swung the sub away from the target and waited...but no explosion shook the night. Both torpedoes obviously had missed. But his target, HMS *Bedfordshire*, gave no evidence of having seen the torpedoes pass or of having detected the sub's presence.

Krech maneuvered into a new firing position. This time the range was down to 600 meters! At 11:40 P.M. the German skipper commanded: Fire three! and once again turned away to await the hit....Seconds ticked by; at the count of thirty-six, a heavy detonation ripped the night open, and the German skipper saw the little vessel hit square amidships. Her stern rose high out of the water and plunged almost instantly from sight. Gunther Krech pulled down his scope, made the entry in his log, and resumed his southward course.[3]

"Two in Civil Air Patrol Lose Lives off New Inlet," *Elizabeth City Daily Advance,* December 26, 1942

Two of North Carolina's gallant sons made the supreme sacrifice in the defense of their Country, when Frank Cooke and J. L. Cooper went down in the breakers off New Inlet Monday evening after their small plane had crashed at about 4:30 o'clock.

The victims were members of the Civil Air Patrol operating out of the Manteo Airport. They left the airport at about 4 o'clock, accompanied by a companion plane and were doing routine scouting for enemy submarines several miles off the coast of Pea Island.

It was nearing dark when the first SOS came in to the local airport. It said, "We are dropping rapidly." Almost before the first message could be translated the second came in saying, "We are dropping rapidly and are going to crash." The instrument must have been left open, for it is reported that the crash could be plainly heard over the receiving station.

The two men cleared the plane and were floating around in their rubber life preservers, according to the pilot of the companion plane. This pilot is reported to have said that he circled around the men and as low as the rough sea would permit him to go in an effort to aid the victims. He and his co-pilot dropped their rubber jackets in the hope it might aid in keeping the struggling men afloat. Darkness and being short of gasoline forced the companion plane to leave, but not until its pilot had done everything possible to rescue the victims.

News of the accident flashed quickly over the telephone and radio, and simultaneously, planes from the airport here and crews from Nags Head, Oregon Inlet, Pea Island and Chicamocomico [*sic*] Coast Guard Stations were desperately trying to get boats through the raging breakers to give succor to the freezing and drowning men.

The evening was bitter cold. No human could withstand the cold for long. The spray that flew over the heads, shoulders and arms of the two men froze almost as soon as it struck them, making them helpless to fight for life. It is reported that one of the men apparently was numb before the companion plane left, as his head was dropped over his shoulder while the life jacket still kept him afloat. The other waived [*sic*] to the companion plane, as its pilot left and headed back to the base.

The horrors of such a death cannot be described in words. First the chilling sensation of being thrown into a wild and vicious ocean with breakers running 20 to 30 feet high, then the biting of the wind as it thrashed the head and shoulders, the pain of suffering from this cold wind and the ice that covered heads and shoulders from the spray which froze as soon as it struck then the weakness and numbness that follows the freezing, the sleepiness, just before which there had been thoughts of home and loved ones and a faint hope that help would come, the wistful scanning [of] the fast darkening horizon for this help, and finally the resignation. The victim has given up. With his resignation comes rest in numbness and sleep and death follows without pain.

While these two men were passing from hope to despair every Naval and Coast Guard unit in this area was striving to rescue them....

It is reported that the Negro crew at Pea Island fought heroically to launch their boats. They were the nearest [to] the scene of the accident. Each time they would thrust their boat into the breakers it would be thrown back at them overturned....

Also seaplanes and airplanes reached the scene of the original accident. It was dark; they let down flares and there was no sight of the men. Such a small object as a man's head bobbing about, first on the crest of the breaker then submerged by its force, then down in the trough, could not very well be spotted over the broad expanse of several square miles, an area that had to be covered on account of the strong tide, which within the hour had probably swept these two men far apart and far from the scene of the tragic crash.

Frank Cooke is survived by his wife and a son, about 14 years old. His home is in Nashville [North Carolina]. J. L. Cooper was unmarried. His home is in Concord. The bodies have not yet been recovered.[4]

A twenty-one-gun salute honors the British sailors from HMS *Bedfordshire* at their burial in 1942.
Courtesy of National Park Service, Cape Hatteras National Seashore

British Cemetery on Ocracoke today
Courtesy of National Park Service, Cape Hatteras National Seashore

Dedication service at the British Cemetery on Ocracoke, December 27, 1942

UNIFORM OF THE DAY:

Officers: Service Blues, white hat cover, with side arms

Enlisted Men: Dress Blues, white hat

Firing Squad: Dress Blues, white hat, with leggings and webbed belts…

AGENDA:

1. 1330—Parade to form in front of Captain Paul Jones Barracks
2. 1340—Parade to proceed to Cunningham Cemetery

   (a) Officers form on left hand side of cemetery facing inward

   (b) Firing squad form on right hand side facing graves

   (c) Support Battalion will form abaft firing squad
3. Protestant Service by Reverend Wm. R. Dixon
4. Catholic Service by Chaplain Donald J. Strange
5. Taps
6. The Salute
7. Retreat
8. At Captain Paul Jones Barracks—Dismissed[5]

Gordon Willis tells Jan Willis Gillikin about the Cape Lookout defenses

WILLIS: In nineteen forty-two or forty-three…they decided they wanted an outpost or an army base down on Cape Lookout…and have patrols go up and down the beach on account of sabbatiers [*sic*] landing.…So they built a nice camp down there. I reckon it had at least one company of men.…They installed two big guns.…And they said those guns had a range of twenty miles.…In addition to those two guns, big guns, on several of the hills around about there, they had what they call machine gun nests. They had rock, sand bags, and most anything like that for protection of the gunners inside there, even gun mounts, machine gun mounts to repel anybody that was trying to come ashore that they didn't want to come ashore. I wouldn't call 'em invaders, but anybody that wasn't welcome, that they didn't want to come ashore, they had the guns and stuff to keep 'em off.…Those guns, they had range. They were big guns. They could have covered right on up as far as, right on past Beaufort Inlet. They had a twenty mile range.

GILLIKIN: When I was a little girl, we'd go to the Cape and I'd see these boats along shore that had washed up that had bullet holes in 'em. What were they?

WILLIS: Oh, those were life boats.

GILLIKIN: Where did they come from?

WILLIS: They come off them big ships.…Submarines were laying offshore of Cape Lookout, enemy subs, German subs…to sink our ships that was carrying supplies over…to England or France or to Russia, wherever. German Subs were there to see how much damage they could do in our shipping lane. And they did quite a bit of damage. They'd torpedo them cargo ships and tankers. And then a lot of times when some of the crew would get off safely in one of the lifeboats, the German Submarine would surface and take a machine gun on deck and kill the survivors that were in boats, instead of lettin' 'em come ashore, you know, safe. They'd shoot 'em right down, right in the boat....

...[The Coast Guard] went out on rescue missions. They rescued quite a few....They'd have to run as silent as they could, without any lights showing until they could get where they thought the designated area was that they were told to go to pick up survivors or whatever. And on one of these trips, Uncle Jimmy [Lewis] told this story. On one of these trips out to pick up survivors, they run their time out and stopped their motor and didn't hear anything. And he told his engineer, or one of the crewman with him, "turn your spotlight on," look around to see if they could see anything. And they said when they turned their spotlight on, they saw the...tower and everything of the German Submarine all afloat out there. He said he hollered at him and said, "turn that light out quick." He told his engineer to crank that engine up and they turned around, and hauled away from there just as fast as they could go. He said he didn't know why the submarine didn't hear 'em or didn't detect 'em, but they didn't. Said that was the scaredest he'd ever been.[6]

Jakie Robertson recalls the day Portsmouth Island was bombed

Being bombed, I remember that in Portsmouth Island....I had nightmares for a long time after that. But they came in, they were making a bombing run and I guess the planes from Cherry Point decided to make a bombing run, and I forgot what island...they thought they were over whenever they made the run....Headlights and stuff out, skeeters were thick and everything. We were just sittin' there and all of a sudden, just flashes and big booms and stuff was goin' off just all around the huntin' lodge and down on the Island, further down the Island and everything. And I was so scared that the next day we walked out there and...you could see the fins. They were just small practice bombs you know, that made a big flash and a big boom so the pilots could get to see where they were hittin'. They didn't really do damage unless they hit something, they'd probably set it on fire, but it went right down the side of the old summer kitchen...and stuck right in the ground, fins stickin' out of the ground after it went off by the summer kitchen, and Uncle Joey dug it out. Then there was one up under the window....It stuck there, and Uncle Tom took it out and they dug those bombs out of the ground and took 'em out. And that was the first time I ever seen Uncle Joey mad. I mean, the man was never, ever...mad at anything.[7]

Naval base on Ocracoke during World War II
Courtesy of The Outer Banks History Center, Manteo, N.C.

O. Lawrence Burnette Jr. pilots a blimp

I received orders to report to the Commanding Officer of the Naval Air Facility, Weeksville, North Carolina. Having never heard of the place before, I soon learned that NAF Weeksville was a blimp base, one of several such lighter-than-air bases on the East Coast, from which blimps patrolled out over the Atlantic searching for German submarines. Now that the war was over, Weeksville was quietly sleeping in the Carolina sun, waiting for the day when it, too, would be retired and closed. Such base closures were commonplace in the draw-down from the war effort.

…No blimps were actually stationed at that time at Weeksville,…[which] was used primarily as an over-night stop-over for blimps cruising up and down the East Coast just for training or to keep sharp flying skills already going dull through lack of use. There were two large, gigantic Quonset-type hangers [sic] on the base which were built to accommodate several blimps during the war, and they were so tall that clouds often formed within them and it rained inside.

…I was assigned to the Weeksville Executive Officer as his Yeoman. The gentleman in that job was Lieutenant Commander Rufus Brinn, USNR….Young for his rank, he was a popular and attractive bachelor, and he seemed to know every eligible young woman in eastern North Carolina. When not partying or dancing, the Commander was drinking, usually at some remote location such as the beach out on the North Carolina Outer Banks….There were two old yellow Stearman bi-planes at Weeksville, for refreshing the blimp pilots in navigation and airmanship, and they were available to the station's flying officers to put in their flying hours to earn their flight pay. Commander Brinn lost no time in making me his co-pilot on his flights, usually crammed into the rear cockpit with half a case of whiskey and a flight helmet of the sort worn by Snoopy of the *Peanuts* comic strip. We would often leave the base about noon, fly out to a remote stretch of the Outer Banks beach, and enjoy the water and the sand while discussing world affairs until Mr. Brinn was too deep in his cups to have a reasonable opinion on the subject. About sundown we would load up and fly back to Weeksville....On one such landing, I noticed we were probably too low for a safe landing, so from the rear cockpit I reached forward and pull[ed] back on the stick and increased the power. After a rough but safe landing, Mr. Brinn with mock seriousness asked me if I had landed the plane.

Loop Shack Hill, Ocracoke, 1944
Courtesy of the Wilmer E. Cochran Collection

"Yes, Sir. I thought one of us should."

"Well, if you are going to fly, you ought to have flight lessons." So Mr. Brinn out of his own pocket paid for me to take flight lessons in a Piper Cub at a local civilian airfield. He also taught me how to fly a blimp whenever one came to visit for a day or two....Actually, it was more like flying a motorized kite than flying an airplane. Those beasts of the air were ungainly, wobbling through the air like a drunken Lighter-than-Air sailor. But they served admirably during the war as platforms from which to hunt for submarines—either boldly dropping a bomb on a sub on the surface (and one or two blimps got shot out of the sky by the subs), or calling in surface ships to prosecute the data. When wearing my half-wing wings [awarded to blimp pilots], I often get asked what they are even by Navy personnel who have never seen such an emblem, or smart-alecks might call attention to the fact that one side of the wings had broken off....I wore, and still proudly when in uniform wear, the Navy wings of gold, even if only half-wings.[8]

U-boat captain Reinhard Hardegen's chance encounter with one of his victims

I was on the thirteenth of January 1942 off New York Harbor, and I saw that it would be a big surprise for the Americans that a submarine will be there....Ships came out of the harbor of New York, and the first night I torpedoed and sank the tanker *Norness*, and she thought at first she hit a mine because the radioman sent a message that they hit a mine. But I sent another torpedo to fulfill my business, and then they remarked that it was a submarine. The second day, I sank the tanker *Coimbra*, all this quite in the range of New York Harbor. But when the papers in the United States said that I was so near New York that I could see Manhattan and the people dancing on the roof of Waldorf-Astoria, that is nonsense....

Then I went southward, and the Americans sank me nearly every day, because we heard radio messages that said, "A submarine sank a tanker, but our air force sank the submarine." And the next day, "Another submarine sank another tanker, but our air force sank also the submarine." On board, we are laughing because there were some airplanes and they dropped also some bombs, but they...were far off. And so I guess for three times I learned by radio that I was sunk. It was always the same submarine, because in Operation Drumbeat we had only five submarines sent over, and only one was [in the area]. It was submarine number 123. That was my submarine.

And then I went on the coast to the south to Cape Hatteras and sank on this patrol a lot of ships. Also, when my torpedoes were out, I sank by artillery.

And on my next patrol, I started at Cape Hatteras and went down to Key West and sank one ship more than on the first patrol. But some of these ships sank in shallow waters, and masts looked out of the water, and they floated these tankers and repaired them, and they were put into service once more but later on sunk by another submarine....

I made a cruise to the Northwest Passage this year [1992], and on board the ship was a man, and he was an able seaman of the tanker *Malay*. I torpedoed this tanker [off Hatteras Island on January 19, 1942,] and also shelled her with guns. And I thought she sank because they gave a message, "We need help. We're sinking quickly." But by him, I learned that they succeeded. They put her aground and also lifted and repaired. And so I met this man fifty years afterwards on a cruise ship in the Northwest Passage.[9]

The Tourist Trade

This chapter taps four favorite subjects from the deep well that is the history of Outer Banks tourism.

Nags Head established itself as North Carolina's first tourist resort by the mid-nineteenth century, after Francis Nixon brought his family to summer there in 1830 to escape "miasmas" back home. Nixon's fellow planters from the mainland coastal counties soon followed his trail to the small sound-side community comprising Nags Head at that time. Hotels and cottages sprang up on the Roanoke Sound shore. Locals who lived a meager existence as fishermen and "wreckers" now found opportunities to sell produce to the newcomers and to convey them across the boardwalk running to the ocean-side beach.

Development on the Atlantic shore began around 1855, when Dr. W. G. Pool of Elizabeth City bought a fifty-acre parcel, divided it into lots, and sold them to acquaintances. Thirteen landmark shingled cottages—the original members of what is called "the Unpainted Aristocracy"—were constructed by 1885. Despite the area's punishing weather, roughly half of those cottages still stand among the thirty-odd structures making up the Nags Head Cottage Row Historic District.

The first piece below is an 1857 snippet from an Elizabeth City paper promoting Nags Head as a tourist destination. The writer's preoccupation with being "molested" by Northern interests suggests that the scent of civil war was already in the air.

The second piece is an obituary for the Nags Head Hotel,

which was built shortly after the Civil War and burned in the summer of 1903. The hotel was constructed partially over Roanoke Sound near Jockey's Ridge.

The next excerpt is a pair of tributes to self-taught carpenter and builder S. J. Twine. Around 1910, Twine was hired to repair and enlarge one of the old Nags Head ocean-side cottages. He went on to upgrade several of the original structures and build more than a dozen of his own, effectively creating the unique Nags Head architectural style immediately recognizable in the historic district, characterized by hip-roofed porches and prop-shuttered windows.

The fourth excerpt concerns the Nags Head Casino, built on the ocean side near the foot of Jockey's Ridge in the early 1930s. The casino was arguably the number-one attraction in northeastern North Carolina through the middle part of the century, drawing upwards of a thousand dancers per weekend night to its second-story ballroom, where they were entertained by acts including Louis Armstrong, Duke Ellington, and Fats Domino. Here, a latter-day performer, Bill Deal of the Rhondels, tells how the crowd at the casino initiated his band's rise to stardom. The casino collapsed following a 1976 storm.

The Lost Colony, another Outer Banks tourist icon, is staged across Roanoke Sound from Nags Head in the Waterside Theatre outside Manteo.

Pulitzer Prize–winning playwright Paul Green was in his office at the University of North Carolina one day during the Depression when he received a visit from W. O. Saunders, editor of the *Elizabeth City Independent*. Saunders, impressed by an outdoor drama he had seen in Bavaria, proposed that Green write a play about the Lost Colony, to be performed on the historic site. Green agreed to attend a preliminary meeting in Manteo.

The project's success was tenuous. The play would be performed by a huge cast—nearly 100 players—in an enormous outdoor theater—2,500 seats. Yet Manteo had a population of 547, and Roanoke Island was reachable from the mainland only via a combination of ferries and dirt roads from either the north or east. The outcome was a testimony to the must-do attitude and public-spiritedness of the New Deal era. The opening-night performance on July 4, 1937—350 years after the events depicted on stage—attracted a full house. President Franklin Roosevelt attended the next month on Virginia Dare's birthday, August 18. Suspended only during the World War II blackout years, the play continues on summer nights to this day as the country's longest-running symphonic drama.

In the first *Lost Colony* piece below, Paul Green reveals how he grew interested in writing about Sir Walter Raleigh's colonists more than a decade before being approached by W. O. Saunders.

In the second, an excerpt from the play, Eleanor Dare (daughter of John White and mother of Virginia Dare) and John Borden (the Everyman character and Eleanor's romantic interest after her husband's death) resolve to abandon Fort Raleigh and lead the colonists to their unknown fate, after they surmise Sir Walter's ships won't be returning for them.

The production boasts some famous alumni, foremost among them Andy Griffith, who played a soldier in 1947 and 1948 before assuming the role of Sir Walter for the next five years. In the final *Lost Colony* piece, National Public Radio personality Carl Kasell tells of the summer he played Wanchese opposite Griffith's Sir Walter. The veteran Griffith was then in his second-last year with the play.

The chapter's next two excerpts concern the father of Ocracoke tourism, Stanley Wahab, who brought the island its first automobile, ice plant, electric plant, fire department, and telephone service. At various times and in various places, he was an oysterman, sailor, accountant, schoolteacher, president of a chain of furniture stores, and operator of an airplane commuter service. The first piece is Ray McAllister's summary of Wahab's accomplishments. The second is his wife's recollection of the time Wahab, always one to make the most of an opportunity, rescued a stranded ship and pocketed forty thousand dollars in the process.

Any treatment of Outer Banks tourism would be lacking without a section on Aycock Brown. A native of Caldwell County in the foothills, Brown became a Banker for life, the story goes, the day he delivered bootleg liquor from Morehead City and saw his future wife standing on the dock at Ocracoke. He was hired as publicity director by the Dare County Tourist Bureau in 1950, at a time when fishing revenues were down and resorts such as Myrtle Beach were investing heavily in promotions. Brown promptly showed an amazing ability to place in major and far-flung publications his ordinary photos of average fishermen holding run-of-the-mill Outer Banks catches, effectively turning a ten-thousand-dollar budget into a million dollars' worth of advertising. His success wasn't a mystery to anyone who met him, propelled as it was by his innumerable acts of generosity and the avalanche of materials he distributed. Known by his loud shirts and banana-boat hats, Brown wrote the well-traveled "Covering the Waterfront" column and took an estimated hundred thousand photos, from disaster pictures to shots of swimsuited local lovelies posed before Outer Banks landmarks. The welcome center at Milepost 1 in Kitty Hawk bears his name. It would be a travesty if it didn't.

The first Aycock Brown excerpt is a portion of a tribute poem by David B. Eisendrath.

The last piece in the chapter is a collection of four snippets of Brown's writing. In the first three, he promotes the Outer

Banks as a destination for fishermen, for wildfowl hunters, and even for refugees after a nuclear holocaust. The fourth snippet shows Brown at his hyperbolic best. The world-record hammerhead shark measured three feet between the eyes and fourteen and a half from nose to tail—a poor specimen indeed beside the twelve-foot-wide, forty-foot-long creature Brown describes.

The *Elizabeth City Sentinel* lauds the Nags Head resort, 1857

We are pleased to hear that Nag's Head is doing well this season, for it is the place for the citizens of this section of North-Carolina to congregate at, where no double-fisted pauper in the livery of a waiter nor yankee abolitionists with their army of saucy negroes to back them, can molest you. But with your own friends and acquaintances, and beyond all, with a fair portion of Carolina's beautiful daughters, you can spend your time as North-Carolinians should. And as you are sojourning under your own "vine and fig tree" none dare molest you for causes that daily transpire at the Northern watering places. Therefore, say we, patronize Nag's Head, and make it what it ought to be—the "Old Point" of North-Carolina.[1]

"Nags Head Hotel Reddens the Heavens with Its Ruin. The Wife of the Proprietor Dies of Excitement," July 27, 1903

Nags Head Hotel was destroyed by fire Sunday evening. Flames suddenly burst from the second story about 6:30 o'clock. An exploding lamp or gasoline stove is supposed to have caused the fire. Practically nothing was saved. The insurance was $4,000.

No lives were lost in the fire. Mrs. Jno. Z. Lowe, wife of the proprietor, died from hemorrhage as a result of over-excitement. Her remains were taken to Norfolk for interment.

Many guests left. There were 140 at the hotel; some domiciled themselves in cottages while others crossed the sound and linger at Manteo. They lost practically all their effects, and some even lost what cash they had on hand, leaving them destitute.

The crew of the United States Life Saving Station nearby rendered all possible assistance.

No future policy has been outlined by the proprietor. He is completely crushed by his bereavement and unable as yet to give thought to business.[2]

Nags Head circa 1900
Courtesy of The Outer Banks History Center, Maneto, N.C.

Two locals remember S. J. Twine, legendary Nags Head cottage builder

CHARLIE REBER:

Old man Twine was the first major builder to dwell in Nags Head. Originally, they were small, boxy camps. He built them to fit the landscape, the slope of the beach. He built the roofline so that as the wind would blow on the roof and raise up off it, it would cause pressure to push down on it, rather than lift them off. It's been told that not one of Mr. Twine's cottages has ever lost a roof or was blown apart....

The houses he built were faced with juniper or cypress shingles—trees that were accustomed to water, so they wouldn't rot. I've replaced a lot of shingles on these houses, but the nails gave out before the shingles did. I built a house with used shingles from these cottages, and all I did was turn them over and renail 'em....

He'd roll the rollers under the houses. There would be rollers on both sides and men on both sides, and they'd stick a pole in the log and would all roll at the same time. He was the first one to move some of the beach houses. He also moved houses from the sound to the ocean. He moved the hotel, of all things—all done by shovel and hand and leveling the dunes if one was in the way.

CLAYTON TWINE:

When I was in junior high school, I helped him build the cottage that now belongs to my sister. It took us three and a half months. It was an eight-by-twelve square box, one room with no bathroom. He bought it and added on to it—two bedrooms and a kitchen downstairs and two bedrooms upstairs. During the week, we ate a spot, a piece of white bread, and a teaspoon of mayonnaise. That was for three meals a day. He was ninety-five years old by then. He laid the whole design out on a pad, the length and width of it; it all came from his head. The roof was sharp-pitched, tin. We were on the roof working right in the sun....It would have killed some young boy today.[3]

The Nags Head Casino launches the Rhondels to stardom, as recalled by Bill Deal

Our band [the Rhondels] had been playing together since we were in college, since about 1959....Beginning around 1965, we would play there [the casino] once every six or seven weeks, rotating with bands like Maurice Williams and the Zodiacs, JoJo and the Frets, and the Rocking Cabanas....

Nags Head Casino with Jockey's Ridge in background
Courtesy of The Outer Banks History Center, Manteo, N.C.

We were a Virginia Beach band....We were what they call a copy band; we'd play the hits, play the beach music, whatever the crowd wanted to hear. It was always packed. We never worried about not having a crowd.

Quite by chance, the crowd wanted to hear this song, "May I?"—a song Maurice Williams wrote and would perform when he was there....But we just didn't play that kind of music up here, that hard-core beach music. I'd heard it before and thought, "We can't do that." It was laid-back beach music.

But you play what the crowd wants to hear, and they wanted

"May I?" We hadn't practiced it. The way we did music back then, I'd listen to it, and I'd sketched out the base line, the horns and piano.…Without even rehearsing it, we did it. I listened to it in the car and wrote out the notes. We used a polka beat, kind of making fun of it and kind of not.

It was almost like a big fraternity and sorority party, and when we played it, the crowd was screaming at us. We looked at each other and thought, "Man, that felt good." We probably played it three times that first night, which was very unusual. We knew maybe twenty-seven songs, so to play one three times, that was different. It felt so good. We decided that night to investigate recording.

That was 1967. That very week, we…recorded "May I?" It was like magic. Nothing else we did really sounded like that.… We printed probably a thousand 45s, and they were gone within a week. We had to go back and print five thousand. Then a distributor called and wanted ten thousand.

By 1968, it was too big for us to handle.…The next thing you know, we had five records that year,…three that charted very well. They were international hits as well.…

The Casino certainly opened doors for a lot of groups.… If you played the Casino, you'd made it.…God bless them for making us do "May I?"[4]

Paul Green on his inspiration for
The Lost Colony

Back in 1921 when I was a student at the University of North Carolina and trying to turn out one-act plays…, I got to thinking about the story of Sir Walter Raleigh's tragic lost colony as subject matter for a play. So I decided to go down to Roanoke Island on the coast and look around at the original site of the colonization attempt.…

It was night when I arrived at the little town of Manteo. I got a room at a local boarding house and early the next morning started walking up the sandy road through the forest toward the place known as Fort Raleigh four miles away. I plodded along in the ankle-deep sand, and the sun was coming up in its great holocaust of flame when I got to the little grove of pines and live oaks on the edge of Croatan Sound and stood beside the small squat stone erected in 1896 to Virginia Dare, the first English child born in the new world. I idly plucked some sassafras twigs and chewed them, and thought upon that band of hardy pioneers who, three hundred and thirty-four years before, had come to this spot to build a fort, a bastion, a beachhead for the extension of the English-speaking empire across the sea....

I thought of the hardships that these people had suffered, of the dark nights, the loneliness, the despair and frustration here, desolate and forgot by Queen Elizabeth in her concern with her Spanish war in England far away. In my mind I could hear the cries of the sick and hungry little children, see the mothers bending above their rough home-made cribs as they twisted and turned in their fever and their fret. And what anguish, what heartache and homesickness! And ever the anxious expectant look toward the eastern sea where never the bright sail of a ship was seen nor the mariner's cheer was heard to tell that help was nigh. Night after night, day after day, only the murmur of the vast and sheeted waters, only the sad whispering of the dark forest to break upon their uneasy dreams.

Yes, here on the very spot where I stood all this had happened, all this had been endured.

I came away charged with inspiration to write a drama on the lost colony.[5]

The Lost Colony, Act 2, Scene 6, in which the colonists resolve to leave Fort Raleigh and meet their destiny

ELEANOR [DARE]. If the ships do not come soon—tomorrow—

[JOHN] BORDEN. They will not come—neither tomorrow nor the next day. I know it now.

ELEANOR (*Quietly.*) And how do you know it?

BORDEN. Rowing the sounds and tramping those endless bogs and wilderness of salt sea grass, my mind worked in a turmoil of fever and fret. Why? Why? Why? I kept asking myself—why has no sign, no word come from the governor and Sir Walter? What could keep them back? Suddenly I saw the answer. How, I know not, but the answer came. England is at war with Spain.

ELEANOR (*Springing up.*) It's true. We should have thought of that.

BORDEN. And the queen keeps back all ships for her defense.

ELEANOR. And may for months to come. Now we must act. Thank God for that. We have supplies in the storehouse to last us but two days at most.

BORDEN. And what would you do?

ELEANOR. If there is game farther south, then we must find it.

BORDEN. And desert the fort?

ELEANOR.…Only if you wish it.…

BORDEN.…Ah, Eleanor, tonight I feel—somehow it was meant to be this way.…And if in the wisdom of God we should be forced to live out our days here forgot and deserted of the world, I should have no regret—none.

ELEANOR (*After a moment—lifting her head bravely.*) Nor I.

BORDEN.…Yea, once Sir Walter said—the victory lieth in the struggle, not the city won.…And so we know—tonight we know. And down the centuries that wait ahead there'll be some whisper of our name—some mention and devotion to the dream that brought us here. Ah—[6]

Carl Kasell recalls performing beside Andy Griffith in *The Lost Colony*

Back in 1952, I was quite active with the high-school drama department back in Goldsboro. We came to Chapel Hill every spring to take part in the high-school drama festival, bring two or maybe three one-act plays for the competition. I was a senior that year.…After the second or third play I was in, the guy who was head of the department, and also was director of *The Lost Colony*, Sam Selden, asked my teacher…if I would read for a new outdoor drama.…And I said, "Sure, I'll do that."

We went to Memorial Hall. He put me in the back of the stage while he stood in the back of the lobby, gave me a script, and said, "Read." Because back then, we didn't use microphones on stage, and in an outdoor arena like they have on Roanoke Island where the play is done, you really have to project. And I learned how to do that.

And that summer, they offered me the part of Chief Wanchese. [The] scene called "the Queen's Garden Scene" is where

Sir Walter Raleigh is presenting two of her new people to the queen. And that was it. I remember before walking on the stage that day in the dress rehearsal, I stood by Andy Griffith, waiting to walk on, and he looked down at me and said, "Carl, you went wild with that paint, didn't you?"

"Too much?"

"Too much. We'll make it a little simpler. I'll show you later how to do it."

And he did. He was a great guy, and he helped me a lot in that play. But that's me, Chief Wanchese. I was the guy in the play itself who caused all sorts of problems because when he came back from England, he found out that the white men had killed his brother, and that caused all sorts of problems. And I had to come out and do something for my dead brother, and that was to attack the fort. That was quite a scene, it really was. I enjoyed it very much. And Andy Griffith was a big, big help.[7]

The 1952 production of *The Lost Colony* featured Andy Griffith as Sir Walter Raleigh and a young Carl Kasell as Wanchese (*lower right corner*).
Courtesy of The Louis Round Wilson Special Collections Library. University of North Carolina at Chapel Hill.

Ray McAllister describes Stanley Wahab

Baltimore businessman Stanley Wahab was the man most responsible for seeing and developing Ocracoke's early tourism potential. Wahab thought Ocracoke was located at "a strategic point on the coast." He began referring to it as "the Bermuda of the United States."

Wahab was born on the island in 1888 and once taught at the local school. But he left a couple of times on his way to becoming president of a chain of furniture stores. Once he returned, he became a dynamo. Wahab opened the Ocean Waves movie theater in 1914 and brought to the island its first automobile, a Hudson Coach.

But it was during the Depression that he began remaking Ocracoke. Wahab built the first water and ice plant, as well as a generator-run electric plant, in the 1930s. He bought Quark's Hammock; it and Green Island were the two hunting clubs on the north side of the island. Wahab opened the Spanish Casino Dance Hall. He bought a 1901 building that one day would become the Island Inn and converted it to a successful coffee shop. His biggest project was the Wahab Village Hotel, a luxury hostelry later renamed Blackbeard's Lodge. One wing included a movie theater; another housed a roller-skating rink. He saw the hotel as part of a "Shores of Contentment" development for tourists. In time, the hotel boasted the island's first electric power and first telephone service.

Wahab also set up a short-lived airplane commuter service. He lobbied for the dredging of Silver Lake and the paving of the road from Hatteras Inlet. He constructed many of the establishments looking toward the ocean beach, making them the first on the island to do so. While islanders always built on the sound side, away from the troublesome Atlantic, Wahab knew the ocean beach would prove the bigger draw for tourists.[8]

The Wahab Village Hotel in the 1950s, when it was called
Blackbeard's Lodge

Myra Wahab captures her husband's entrepreneurial spirit in his rescue of a stranded ship

The last ship that was wrecked here was the *Charlie Mason*, and that was in 1948. And Mr. Wahab did get it off [the shoals]. It belonged to the Smith Brothers in Morehead City, and he happened to be in the office down there talking to the man whose father owned the boat. The man said, "That's my father's favorite of all our boats," and that he would give $40,000 cash for that boat in Ocracoke Harbor. Mr. Wahab said, "Put it in writing and I'll get the boat off." So they signed the contract, and at that time he leased the airport in Manteo and had planes. He had the planes fly to Baltimore and pick up big sea anchors.... They put the anchors out in the sea, and everytime [*sic*] they'd have a high tide, they'd take the slack off. And then, of course, the tide would ebb and they'd get it settled down.

They worked on it about a week or 10 days, floated it, brought it into the harbor here, and then it was taken down to Morehead City.[9]

David B. Eisendrath's "Tribute to Aycock"

From Ocracoke to Manteo,
From inlet to the town,
The word is sped, the news is fed
By hustling Aycock Brown.

Were triplets born in Hatteras?
Did sailors wreck and drown?
The news is quickly gathered
And sent on by Aycock Brown.

How big a marlin was weighed in?
With polished verb and noun
The dispatches are flashed world-wide
By dashing Aycock Brown.[10]

An Aycock Brown sampler

ON FISHING:

Oregon Inlet channel bass fishing is better so far this season than it has been since 1947, according to sportfishing observers who have roles in one of the Dare Coast's major attractions—the Spring run of channel bass....

Capt. Kenneth Ward, skipper of the cruiser *Cherokee*, reported this week that to date, during the current season considerably more channel bass have been taken than were landed during a similar period in 1948....One party of Virginians fishing with him last weekend landed 19 of the copper colored beauties in one day.[11]

ON WILDFOWL HUNTING:

Many young hunters who came to Northeastern North

Carolina for the opening of the 1949 migratory wildfowl season are enjoying the best goose and duck shooting of their lifetimes. Oldtimers [*sic*], some of whom can recall the market-hunting days which were outlawed early in this century, reported that this season there were more wildfowl and better shooting than since the late '20s....

Some of the hunters had their limit within an hour after the season officially opened. Others who remained out until sunset returned to their bases on shore with good kills. Just about every species of duck was killed here on the Dare coast including redheads, canvasbacks, widgeons, pintails and black mallards. One hunter reported more curlew, willet, snipe and swan in the Oregon Inlet section this year than in his lifetime.[12]

ON "EAST CAROLINA—HAVEN FROM ATOM ATTACK":

The Sunday morning newspaper here [Norfolk, Virginia] carried a story under the following caption: "East Carolina—Haven From Atom Attack."...

Temporary housing could and would probably be set up in the small communities between Norfolk and Elizabeth City—between Norfolk and Nags Head, Manteo....The matter is so serious that local defense chiefs are to confer with Eastern Carolina officials in the near future to map plans which everyone hopes may never be placed into effect—but which would be very necessary when and if an enemy of this nation should happen to drop a few atom bombs on Norfolk, the biggest naval center on the east coast and also one of the most important ports.

...All of the sons of Norfolk are looking...to Northeastern North Carolina, where it may be necessary to go and in a hurry should World War III, that seems in the offing, with the preliminaries getting hotter and hotter in Korea, become a reality....

One of the most important things to do after the attack here would be to move people out of town—and the only way they can be moved quickly is to move them into the sparsely settled northeastern North Carolina area.[13]

ON THE LEGENDARY HATTERAS HAMMERHEAD:

They still talk about the biggest hammerhead shark ever seen at Hatteras and through the years the story has become legend. Never before nor since has such a whopper been seen anywhere.

The late Fred Stowe used to tell the story about the time General Billy Mitchell heard about the big shark, was first skeptical and then amazed when told the details.

"He asked me one day what was the largest shark I had ever seen," said Stowe.

"It measured 12 feet from eye to eye. It was a hammerhead that someone caught near a reef in Pamlico Sound and brought in to the docks," Stowe told the General....

Lloyd Styron, another Hatteras resident, had heard the story of the big hammerhead. He figured that if its eyes were 12 feet from one to the other, that the length must have been 40 feet or more, and the width of the queer shaped hammer-like heads are usually about one-fourth the length of their body.[14]

By Sea, Land, and Air

The Outer Banks boasts many positives, but ease of access isn't among them. Depending on the age and sleep status of the children in one's party, reaching the islands can be the adventure of a lifetime or medieval-caliber torture.

Access by water is the most romantic and time-honored means. Today's Outer Banks ferry operation is a public-private hybrid. As part of the nation's second-largest state-run ferry system, the North Carolina Department of Transportation operates the boats on the major Cedar Island–Ocracoke, Swan Quarter–Ocracoke, and Hatteras-Ocracoke routes, as well as an emergency route between Stumpy Point and Rodanthe and the Currituck–Knotts Island route near the Virginia border. Captain Toby Tillett, who ran a tug and barge service across Ocracoke Inlet beginning in the mid-1920s, is considered the father of the ferry system. The state began subsidizing him in the 1930s and finally bought him out in 1950. The largest ferries carry up to fifty vehicles and three hundred passengers; Hatteras-Ocracoke is the most-traveled route. Private ferry service has existed at least since Wilbur Wright rode the *Curlicue* from Elizabeth City to Kitty Hawk in 1900 during his first Outer Banks sojourn. Wilbur nearly drowned in the process; today's options are immeasurably improved. Private ferries provide access to the less-traveled portions of the Banks, most notably to various parts of Cape Lookout National Seashore.

The first two excerpts below are accounts of water travel to the Outer Banks. The first describes a 1950s trip aboard the

Dolphin, last in the long line of Ocracoke mailboats, which carried freight and passengers in addition to postal parcels, and whose arrivals at Silver Lake were daily social events. In the piece, the *Dolphin* transfers mail to a skiff manned by one of the aging citizens of Portsmouth Village, which would be abandoned by 1971. Mailboat service ended in 1964. In the second piece, Barbara Brannon talks with the captain and crew of the *Gov. Edward Hyde*, which traveled the two-and-a-half-hour Swan Quarter–Ocracoke route beginning in the late 1970s.

Most Outer Banks visitors arrive via the U.S. 158 Wright Memorial Bridge across Currituck Sound to Southern Shores or the U.S. 64 Virginia Dare Memorial Bridge across Croatan Sound to Roanoke Island, then the Washington Baum Bridge across Roanoke Sound to the Nags Head vicinity. The next several pieces treat transportation by sand, road, and bridge.

The third and fourth excerpts are portions of interviews with beach-driving brothers Anderson and Stocky Midgett. In 1938, their father, Theodore Stockton Midgett Sr., purchased a bus and freight franchise to run between Manteo and Hatteras Village. He soon died of a heart attack, leaving sons Harold, eighteen, Anderson, thirteen, and Stocky, ten, with a Ford station wagon and a vision. The young brothers created a remarkable legacy, canceling only about twenty trips over two and a half decades and wearing out the Ford and forty-odd other vehicles ranging from Jeep-like conveyances to converted trucks to buses. The journey began at eight each morning in Hatteras Village, from which point the brothers picked up passengers and freight in Frisco, Buxton, Avon, Salvo, Waves, and Rodanthe, then ferried across Oregon Inlet and continued to Manteo, then returned all the way home. When the bus floundered, as frequently happened, the passengers pushed. Rides with young Stocky were the most hair-raising; driving barefoot and either standing at the wheel or sitting on a pillow, he hit speeds of up to forty-five on the sand. Anderson and Stocky later helped found Cape Hatteras National Seashore and ran a successful real-estate business.

Governor Melville Broughton (center) assists with pushing one of the cars in his motorcade out of the sand during his inspection of the Cape Hatteras Lighthouse.
Courtesy of The Outer Banks History Center, Maneto, N.C.

The next piece is a slice-in-time look at the problems besetting N.C. 12, the vital but washout-prone main artery down the Outer Banks. The snippets from the North Carolina Department of Transportation's "Rebuilding N.C. 12" blog detail repair efforts on a bit of road on northern Hatteras Island after Hurricane Sandy in 2012. The Banks portion of N.C. 12 runs from Corolla through Ocracoke Island.

In the following piece, Glenn McVicker offers a lifetime's

worth of memories of the Bonner Bridge, another Outer Banks flashpoint. Now more than two decades beyond its projected lifespan, the bridge is victimized by both age and the ever-changing Oregon Inlet beneath it. Ongoing public discussions and legal actions attend its possible improvement or replacement.

In the final excerpt, private pilot and blogger Chris Houston details an idyllic day of flying the Outer Banks. He, his wife, and their daughter (nicknamed "The Bear") depart First Flight Airport near Wright Brothers National Memorial for an afternoon playing on the Ocracoke sand. En route, he describes numerous Outer Banks landmarks from the air. In addition to the facilities at Kill Devil Hills and Ocracoke, pilots have access to Dare County Regional Airport in Manteo and Billy Mitchell Airport in Frisco.

Riding the Ocracoke mailboat, as recalled by Carl Goerch

The name of the craft that carried the mail last year was the *Dolphin*, captained by Ansley O'Neal. She's about forty-five feet in length....

During the summer months the mail boat will carry as many as thirty-five passengers. At other times there may be only four or five aboard.

In addition to mail and passengers, the boat also hauls considerable freight. This is stowed away in the hold and on deck.

There are benches on which you can sit with a fair degree of comfort. If the boat is crowded, you can find a resting place on an empty fish box or take your seat on some of the packages of freight. If it starts raining, everybody tries to get down in the cabin. Those who are unsuccessful in doing this cheerfully remain on deck and get soaked.

There's usually an awning over the afterdeck. If you can't get under the awning you stand a fine chance of getting one of the best sunburns you've ever had.

Doesn't sound particularly appealing, does it? However, I don't believe I've ever heard of anybody complaining. Everybody seems to enjoy the trip.

When the mail, the passengers and the freight have been stowed aboard, the boat backs away from the dock and heads out into Core Sound. Over on the outer banks you can see the Coast Guard station. On your left, about half an hour after you leave Atlantic, is Cedar Island....

The distance from Atlantic to Ocracoke is slightly less than thirty miles, air line. The water route, however, is considerably farther than that, due to the twisting channels.

The boat approaches Portsmouth, the island just below Ocracoke. Half a mile out from shore stands a Negro man in a skiff. The Post Office Department hires him to meet the boat every trip and take the mail ashore. The water is so shallow that the mail boat itself cannot get any closer to the little pier at Portsmouth.

The Negro's name is Henry Picott and he receives a salary of $50 a month for this little job.

There are only seventeen people living on Portsmouth Island. Most of them are old and rather feeble. As a matter of fact, Henry, age 59, is the youngest man there....

The boat crosses Ocracoke Inlet and proceeds up the sound side of Ocracoke Island, about a half-mile from shore. Three or four sand dunes on our right. Then the village, with the lighthouse and Coast Guard station dominating the scene...

The mail boat is due at about 3:30. Shortly after three o'clock people begin to gather at the dock in front of the post office or in the stores just a short distance away....

Usually it's some small boy, perched precariously on a piling at the end of the pier, who is first to glimpse the boat swinging around the point and getting ready to come in through the narrow entrance of the harbor.

"Here she comes!" he calls out.

People leave the stores. They rise from the boxes or crates on which they have been sitting and begin walking out on the pier....

The boat swings slowly up alongside the dock and is made fast. Suitcases and other baggage are thrown out. Passengers clamber over the low railing and onto the pier....

There's a general stirring around as baggage is claimed and the mail is taken to the post office. Suitcases are loaded into waiting vehicles. Gradually the crowd moves over to the post office. The mail is put up in short order. Trucks and jeeps move off. People begin to walk away. Soon the crowd has dispersed entirely and the big event of the day is over.[1]

Hatteras Inlet ferry, circa 1940s
Courtesy of The Outer Banks History Center, Manteo, N.C.

Barbara Brannon hobnobs with the crew of the ferry *Gov. Edward Hyde*

On the long Swan Quarter–to–Ocracoke route, mate W. G. Mason, a wiry, sixty-something-looking fellow with a glint of humor in his eye, takes a moment to talk to me about the boat's operation. Who are the passengers, mainly? In the summer, mostly tourists, he says. But in the winter it's largely locals who have business on the mainland. Commuters who work at the phosphate plant in Aurora, for instance, or at the air base....

Mason takes me up to the bridge to speak with Capt. L. M. Mason—no relation—who, after phoning in to headquarters to clear my credentials, is pleased to show me the vessel's state-of-the-art navigation system.

A computer map much like the one on your home television screen shows the weather in the region. The officers also call in regularly to the NOAA weather station at Newport, N.C., and send in their own weather reports three or four times daily.

Two hazards, the captain says, are the ever-present crab pots and the shrimp boats, which maintain relatively stationary positions as they work, in contrast to the steadily moving ferry. "The best place for the crab pots is on the slope from the shallows to the channel," he explains. If lines should foul the ferryboat's propellers, the crew would have to get a diver to go under and make repairs in port.

The crew on this route works twelve hours on, twelve hours off for seven-day shifts, alternating with seven days off. Their morning routine begins with the deck personnel checking to see that the boat is ready: they start the generators (after the boat has been connected to shore electricity at night) and get the main engines going. The chief calls up to the pilot house, which then takes control of the vessel. The captain fires up the electronic gear—radars, depth finder, radio, and the like.

Up on the bridge, the officers have a clear view on nearly all sides and an impressive array of instruments. There are two steering systems (really four, since the boat can be steered with a lever if needed). There is also an alarm system for the boat's below-deck compartments, to show which are open. The computer-screen chart is connected to GPS, which records position dynamically throughout the passage. Fancy electronics notwithstanding, the captain still keeps a paper log.

The boat is powered by two 850-horsepower main engines, capable of delivering a speed of 12.5 knots. Averaging 10 knots, it takes 550 gallons of fuel per day to make four crossings. "You burn more fuel if you have to run harder, just like a car," explains Captain Mason.

Engineer R. A. Graham comes into the pilot house and joins the conversation. How about night navigation? I ask the men. There are buoys to mark the channel, they explain, but the crew also rely on radar. Powerful lamps can be directed toward water or land as needed, and help in docking after dark.

When it comes to dealing with passengers, the crew have learned through years of experience what to watch out for. If a driver is gripping the steering wheel tightly with both hands, says mate W. G. Mason, that's bad. "You see their muscles tense up." He rolls his eyes to indicate the potential consequences. "Or you see them driving up talking on their cell phones."

Other onboard difficulties include dead batteries—as when a traveler leaves the car radio on for two hours. But by far the most common problem is keys locked in the car. "I hear car alarms go off," says the captain. "My mind is attuned to anything out of the ordinary." And he's gone so far as to get on the PA system and remind his passengers, "Nobody will steal your car on this ferry"—or if they do, they won't get very far.

I ask what kind of vehicles the ferry can transport. "Most people don't realize what's involved" in the ferries' cargo, says

W. G. Mason. Captain Mason chimes in: "After Hurricane Isabel [in 2003], we had to bring over everything that was needed on the island for repairs: big trucks, rocks, everything." The Sound Class ferries can carry 300 passengers, but vehicle capacity varies depending on the type of vehicles. Fuel trucks, for instance, still have to call ahead to get clearance for a special run, and military convoys arrange transportation in advance.

Mate Mason can't resist another anecdote. He parrots the British accent of one passenger who approached him and said, "I'm afraid I've locked my keys in my car." The crew offered assistance in jimmying the lock, but to no avail. The passenger studied the situation for a moment. "Is that your chief stoker?" he asked Mr. Mason, referring to the engineer.

"Have him take a hammer and knock the window out," the man directed, resigning himself to the necessity. "I don't mind paying to have it replaced, but it sure buggers the air conditioning."[2]

Anderson Midgett recalls driving the Manteo-Hatteras beach bus

My daddy and his son Stockton Harold Midgett started the bus line July 28th, 1938, and we ran that bus line for 35 [*sic*] years until after the [Bonner] bridge was built in 1963, and we continued to run it until 1965, I believe. We traveled up all through where the refuge [Pea Island National Wildlife Refuge] is, across the ferry at Oregon Inlet, proceeded on into Manteo, making one round trip each day. We had no roads as such, so you went anywhere you could make a track and gradually build your own roads. You traveled on dirt all the way through the refuge, through the whole island, and the first highway you saw was when you got to what they called the Whalebone, right outside of Manteo just a few miles.…The first highway we got down on Hatteras Island was in '54, and that was put in from Hatteras to Avon, then they gradually got us connected on up into Manteo....

There were a lot of different tracks. A lot of times, they all led into one in certain areas, depending on how the beach was. And if a track got too bad, then you moved over and built your other tracks. Now sometimes we went up the surf on low tides....Everybody was driving it, it wasn't only the bus line. They had mail trucks, freight trucks, they had trucks bringing supplies in that were going up and down there one and two times a week. There were cars every day.[3]

Theodore Stockton "Stocky" Midgett relives his glory days as a barefoot, undersized bus jockey

I started driving the bus quite a bit when I was 10 years old. I didn't drive the full trip sometime, but I filled in as a relief driver and with my brothers. But I started when I was around 10 years old, and as everybody used to say, "He always had to sit on a pillow, either that or look through the steering wheel."

The Midgett brothers' bus service ran from Manteo to Hatteras.
Courtesy of Midgett Family Heirs

But I managed to drive it and drove it quite frequently. And I have had help from the park service and help from the fish and wildlife, and I've also helped them several times.

It was more or less everybody helped everybody else. If we were stuck, the passengers would get out and push, and also if a park ranger came along, he would help, and everybody had to help one another because it wasn't a freeway to travel. In other words, you had to depend on your neighbors and your friends to help.... There were no regulations at the time. We did not have to have even any license on the busses, nor neither did I have any driver's license....

I delivered mail and picked up things for the members of the Coast Guard. In fact, I sometimes even had lunch with them and also at Pea Island, which was one of the friendlier stations on the Island, which was all colored at that time. They traveled with me quite a bit back and forth, and they were always welcomed, and we were always welcomed into their station, and they were always glad to help anyway [*sic*] possible.... Before the road went in, we had the mail franchise, and we delivered to each and every post office on the Island, as well as we would drop mail off to some of the Coast Guard Stations, and we picked up packages for the people at the Coast Guard Stations. Also, we delivered a daily newspaper which was the *Virginian Pilot*....

People knew what time we normally would come through and they'd be out by the road. Also, when we came up to areas where we knew people would normally be, we would honk our horns. People just knew.

We were the only public transportation on the Island up to Manteo. There were private cars, and they sometimes could have problems in the sand. Most folks didn't have four wheel drive. It was expensive, and we knew how to drive.[4]

Construction of the Herbert C. Bonner Bridge
Courtesy of The Outer Banks History Center, Manteo, N.C.

Excerpts from the NCDOT's "Rebuilding N.C. 12" blog

DECEMBER 5, 2012

Calm weather conditions have prevailed in Dare County and our crews have made significant repairs to N.C. 12.... This will be a multi-step process that will include installing sandbags, reconstructing dunes, and rebuilding the road near Rodanthe where Hurricane Sandy and a pair of Nor'easters damaged the highway.

Crews are currently placing 15-foot-long sandbags along a 0.4-mile section of N.C. 12 at the S-Curves just north of Rodanthe on Pea Island. In all, 1,800 new sandbags will go in to create a protective barrier between the ocean and the road. Once the sandbags are in place, we'll rebuild the dunes on top of the sandbags.

DECEMBER 18, 2012

Today, one of our engineers remarked that he'd never seen anything as beautiful as crews putting down asphalt on the section of N.C. 12 north of Mirlo Beach damaged by Hurricane Sandy and twin Nor'easters....

Folks who live, work and like to visit Rodanthe and places south have had to access those beloved spots via four-wheel drive vehicles or the emergency ferry route for weeks. It hasn't been easy—that we know.

But, the sight of heavy equipment putting down fresh asphalt to rebuild this road that serves as a vital lifeline for so many offers the promise that all the hardship is about to end....

...We're confident that we can achieve our goal of reopening the highway on or by Dec. 25. What a great Christmas gift that will be!

JANUARY 16, 2013

As of right now, no work is going on N.C. 12 at Mirlo Beach because of a mechanical issue with the dredge pump. The pump is not generating enough pressure to keep its lines from clogging with sand. A part needed to fix the issue has been ordered and will be shipped overnight. The repair is expected to be made tomorrow.

JANUARY 22, 2013

Sandbag installation is now complete along the part of N.C. 12 just north of Mirlo Beach that was damaged during Hurricane Sandy and a pair of Nor'easters last year. The final 41 sandbags were put into place on Monday, Jan. 21, connecting the section of sandbags from the north end to the section at the south end. The total number of sandbags placed along this section of N.C. 12 is 2,048.

MARCH 26, 2013

On March 19, Governor Pat McCrory declared a state of emergency for N.C. 12 in Dare County to help the N.C. Department of Transportation move ahead with a short-term solution to protect the critical coastal highway from frequent ocean overwash caused by high winds and strong surf....

"The people there have real concerns about the road they depend on to get to work, school or medical appointments," said Governor McCrory. "They need a highway that is not forced to close every time a storm approaches."[5]

Glenn McVicker's Bonner Bridge memories

I am on top of the world, and there's no place to pull over and stop. The Herbert C. Bonner Bridge, which crosses Oregon Inlet on the Outer Banks, serves the same purpose as all other bridges—it's meant to carry you from one piece of land to the next. But to me, this is the finest scenic overlook in North Carolina. The apex is six stories above the water, the ocean to the east and the sound to the west, with only strips of sand north and south, a piece of man's concrete coursing over some of the most untamable natural terrain in the state....

My first trip across Oregon Inlet was on a ferry. I was 7 years old when my family took our first vacation to the Outer Banks in my parents' 1958 Chevy Brookwood Station Wagon. This was its first big trip, and its colors matched the inlet's colors. The exterior was dark blue-green, the shade of the deepest water, and the interior was aqua green, matching the shallows.

As we pulled aboard, I pretended I was taking a ship to sea. I asked my dad if this was like the Liberty ship he rode to England with the U.S. Army trucks. "Well, not exactly," he said. "This smells a lot better."

The next time I crossed the inlet, the bridge was there.

It was 1973, and I was 21 years old, driving my 1962 Ford

Falcon Club Wagon. The van was a mess, boxy and ugly. Orange and white and looking much like a crab-pot float, the van would have looked better on the old ferry.

The bridge, meanwhile, was flowing and dramatic, like a modern sculpture. The flat nose of the Club Wagon brought the view inches from my hands on the wheel....

Nowadays, I make it to the Outer Banks and across the Bonner Bridge often, driving my 25-year-old Volvo 240 Wagon. I have put more than 470,000 miles on my trusted, rusted haul-all, most of them along the North Carolina coast.

More than ever, I look forward to each crossing and to looking down upon the ever-changing drama below. Heading south, the Bonner Bridge starts by running low over the marshes and beach, then begins to rise toward the main shipping-channel span. To the left, I see the first bold view of the Atlantic Ocean. The south end of Bodie Island bends under the bridge. Breakers roll into the mouth of the inlet, and the water changes color as it shallows. Ahead on the north end of Pea Island is a restored building that once housed a U.S. Coast Guard station now overrun by the southerly migration of the inlet.

Now near the top, the view goes on for miles down Hatteras Island. Here it's easy to realize how narrow and fragile this ribbon of sand actually is....

Sometimes, if there's no traffic approaching from behind, I stop at the top. From this spot, the 360-degree view is new every time, the ever-moving waters always in control of the scenery. Suddenly, I don't miss the familiar North Carolina land. I'm simply in awe....

The Bonner is a disputed bridge. Dredging issues cause problems underneath and safety issues up above. It's not an old bridge, but it's not young anymore, either....

I hear there is going to be a new bridge. That's good. It

needs to happen. The Bonner Bridge was built in 1963, and it was made to last 30 years. The folks out here I know need the bridge for their livelihood. But for those of us who just pass through, a new bridge will be good for us, too. It will be a reminder that we must progress. I'll be ready, with another car for another bridge, and every time I cross, I'll be looking for another opportunity to slow down, maybe stop, and enjoy the view.[6]

A private pilot flies the Outer Banks

In the early 1700s, the idyllic vacation spots of North Carolina's Outer Banks were havens for pirates. Notorious corsair Edward Teach, best known by the fearsome nickname "Blackbeard," was fond of mooring his ships in the deep inlets off the southern tip of Ocracoke Island. It was here that he eventually met his demise, permanently intertwining his story with that of Ocracoke.

Kristy, The Bear (as in "don't poke the…"), and I departed from First Flight Airport late in the afternoon, having completed our pilgrimage to aviators' hallowed ground, where the Wright Brothers first tamed the ether with powered, controllable flight. Ocracoke Island was our next destination. Sadly, we did not bring any puffy shirts with us; our ordinary nonbuccaneer garb would have to suffice.

On departure, our single-engine airplane bore us steadfastly through mechanical turbulence generated from gusty winds sweeping through trees around First Flight Airport. Once above the treeline, the air calmed significantly. We stayed over the western shore of the islands, proceeding south with Kitty Hawk and Nags Head passing beneath our port wing.

The massive fishing piers of the Outer Banks make the comparatively diminutive piers back home on the Great Lakes seem ridiculously inadequate. The black and white lighthouses of the Outer Banks are iconic. We flew past the Bodie Island Lighthouse on our way to Ocracoke. Bodie and Pea Islands are connected by the Oregon Inlet Bridge, which I recognized from an earlier sojourn into the Outer Banks.

When following such a narrow strip of earth surrounded on both sides by seawater, navigation is easy-peasey. The Outer Banks are unlike any other place we have visited by airplane. We navigated according to a chart unlike anything ever used by Blackbeard or his contemporaries. On first inspection, it is a bewildering superposition of restricted airspace annotated with arcane incantations like "Request status of R-5313 A, B, C, D from GIANT KILLER on 118.125." The wildlife refuge areas around the islands necessitate flight above 2,000 feet, and the Pamlico MOA (military operations area) overlies the islands at 8,000 feet. Provided that one stays over the islands and within the aforementioned altitude bounds, navigating the region is a non-event.

The distinctive tip of Cape Hatteras was easy to recognize. We turned southwest to continue along Hatteras Island toward Ocracoke. The Cape Hatteras Lighthouse is the tallest brick lighthouse in the United States and stands vigil over a particularly hazardous region of sea known as the "Graveyard of the Atlantic." In 1999, an eroding beach forced a move of the entire lighthouse complex 2,900 feet inland.

Ocracroke Island is one of the more remote places in the Outer Banks. It lies approximately 16 nautical miles off the mainland and, unlike many of the islands, is not connected by any bridges. The island can only be reached by boat or airplane. From above, we observed ferries cross paths as they carried passengers and vehicles between Ocracoke and Hatteras.

Ocracoke Island Airport lies directly—conveniently—off the beach. Our plan was to get a ride to Howard's Pub, whose website advertises that they actively monitor the airport's Unicom frequency and will pick up customers after landing. We landed in a stout crosswind off the ocean and taxied to the crowded aircraft parking apron, maneuvering our airplane into the last available parking spot.

From the modest airport office, we called Howard's Pub to arrange a ride for a late lunch. Our chariot arrived within minutes: a street-legal six-seat electric car. The driver delivered us to the pub by pulling into a narrow car port bearing the sign "Limo Parking."

Reading the menu, we learned that the Howard family has deep roots in Ocracoke. William Howard was Blackbeard's quartermaster. Our late lunch/early dinner was good, though we realized that we were all a bit dehydrated when we each drained several glasses of lemonade in short order. For entertainment, The Bear was provided with crayons, an activity book, and food served upon a Howard's Pub Frisbee.

Back at Ocracoke Island Airport, we learned that our airplane can serve as an adequate cabana for changing into your swimsuit provided that you are six years old. Otherwise, it is perhaps not the best choice (a little too small and a little too public). Once The Bear was changed, we strolled off airport property and directly onto the beach, a rare novelty for us.

The Bear enjoyed finding sea shells along the pristine beach. But mostly, I think she delighted in playing in the surf. Kristy and I waded out with her for much of the time. At one point, a large wave soaked my shorts, so I retired above the tide line to dry off and watch The Bear frolic in the sea.

As the sun crept closer to the western edge of the world, it was time to take flight from Ocracoke Island. Convincing The Bear to leave the water and return to the air took a bit of effort.

We departed Ocracoke. Climbing parallel to the shore, we noticed that the beach had emptied out significantly. Tire marks tracing the paths of beachgoers' vehicles branched out across the beach from a nearby access road, a striking sight from our aerial perch.

We turned back over the barrier islands to retrace our course to First Flight. We flew past the town of Hatteras, this time staying east of the beach. The Cape Hatteras Fishing Pier, also known as the Frisco Pier, has been beset by natural disasters and remained closed since 2008. It reached out from the shoreline in a broken line, isolated portions of the once contiguous structure now man-made islands standing above the waves. "I would *not* want to go out on that!" remarked The Bear as we flew past.

As the westering sun neared the horizon, it reflected from the surface of Pamlico Sound and infused the world with a golden luster. Details in Oregon Inlet stood out in stark contrast against this early evening sun.

The mainland could be seen in the distance, connected to Roanoke Island by the Virginia Dare Memorial Bridge. The Washington Baum Bridge connects Roanoke Island to Nags Head, just south of Kill Devil Hills. It was a route that I drove two years prior, this time seen from a profoundly different perspective. Moments later, we were back to where our Outer Banks sojourn began, flying over the impressive Wright Brothers Memorial. From there, we set a course to Chesapeake, Virginia, thus ending our day-long adventure in the former haunts of pirates and pioneering airmen.[7]

Acknowledgments

I owe thanks to Carolyn Sakowski, who lit a fire under my nethers (figuratively, of course) when this project languished, sought out excerpts and photos, and untangled the mess that was my original Notes section; Sally Johnson, who gathered permissions far and wide; Artie Sparrow, who wore out a library card on my behalf and stood strong when the overdue-book police came calling; Sarah Downing, former assistant curator at the Outer Banks History Center, who made time to read my chapters while transitioning to her new position at the Western Regional Archives in Asheville, North Carolina; BJ Mountford, who generously and on short notice wrote an original piece for this volume; Chris Houston, who reworked his blogpost to better suit my purposes; Karen McCalpin, executive director of the Corolla Wild Horse Fund, for promptly sending materials; Michael Rikard, former chief of resource management at Cape Lookout National Seashore, for mailing a CD of oral histories that proved invaluable; Tama Creef, archivist at the Outer Banks History Center, for materials related to Frank and David Stick; the librarians in the North Carolina Room at the Forsyth County Public Library and the North Carolina Collection in the Wilson Library at UNC–Chapel Hill; all those who granted permission for the use of excerpts and photos; and the lovely Mary Kirk, who found a couple of my favorite pieces in the book.

John F. Blair, Publisher, would like to thank the following people for their assistance in gathering photographs and permissions:

Cyndy Holda from the National Park Service; William A. Owens Jr., William (Bill) H. Brown, Kim Andersen, and Sarah Downing from the State Archives of North Carolina; Sandra Harris and Katie Mosher from N.C. Sea Grant; Laura Gribbin and Victoria Wells from the University of North Carolina Press; Jackie M. Rose from the *Philadelphia Inquirer*; Adam Ferrell from The History Press; Irene Nolan from the *Island Free Press*; Rachel Duane from *Our State* magazine; Gary Montalbine from the Knotts Island Scrapbook; William Cross from North Carolina State University; Mike Goodman from the *Daily Advance*; Lisa Crawley from NCDOT Communications Office; America Star Books Support Team; Ursula Barkers from the *Daily Press*; Karen McCalpin from the Corolla Wild Horse Fund; Steven Neshkoff from the National Park Service; Hunter Bretzius from the *Gaston Gazette*; Aaron Tuell, Outer Banks Visitor Center; Amy Howard, Ocracoke Preservation Society; David Krueger, National Park Service; Stuart Parks, The Outer Banks History Center; Beth Midgett, Midgett Realty; Clayton C. Shortridge; Barbara A. Brannon; Susan Van Dongen; Terry M. Parkerson; Melinda Lukei; Lawrence Burnette; Ray McAllister, and Susan Rountree.

Notes

SIR WALTER'S LEGACY

[1] "Charter to Sir Walter Raleigh, 1584," in *The Federal and State Constitutions, Colonial Charters, and Other Organic Laws of the States, Territories, and Colonies Now or Heretofore Forming the United States of America*, compiled and edited by Francis Newton Thorpe (Washington: GPO, 1909).

[2] Arthur Barlowe, "The first voyage made to the coast of America...," in *A General Collection of the Best and Most Interesting Voyages and Travels in Various Parts of America,* vol. 2, by John Pinkerton (Longman, Hurst, Rees, Orme and Brown, 1819), 565, 566, 570.

[3] Edmund Goldsmid, ed., *The Voyages of the English Nation to America,* compiled by Richard Hakluyt, vol. 2 (London: E. & G. Goldsmid, 1889), 301.

[4] Thomas Hariot, *A Briefe and True Report of the New Found Land of Virginia*...(New York: J. Sabin & Sons, 1871), 16.

[5] Ibid., 45.

[6] Charles K. True, *The Life and Times of Sir Walter Raleigh, Pioneer of Anglo-American Colonisation* (New York: Nelson & Phillips, 1877), 62–63.

[7] John White, "The Fourth Voyage Made to Virginia, in the Yere 1587," in *Early English and French Voyages: Chiefly from Hakluyt, 1534–1608*, by Richard Hakluyt (Charles Scribner's Sons, 1906), 290–93.

[8] John Lawson, *The History of Carolina, Containing the Exact Description and Natural History of That Country*...(London: W. Taylor and J. Baker, 1714), 62.

BLACKBEARD AND FRIENDS

[1] Amy Crawford, "The Gentleman Pirate," Smithsonian.com, July 31, 2007, www.smithsonianmag.com/biography/the-gentleman-pirate-159418520/. Accessed July 11, 2014.

[2] Charles Johnson (Daniel Defoe), *A General History of the Pyrates* (London: T. Warner, 1724), 87.

[3] Ibid., 12–14.

[4] Ibid., 77.

[5] Ibid., 145.

[6] *The Tryals of Major Stede Bonnet & Other Pirates* (London: printed for Benj. Cowse at the Rose & Crown in St. Paul's Church-yard, 1719), 37-43.

[7] Alexander Spotswood to the Council of Trade and Plantations (London), Dec. 22, 1718, in *Calendar of State Papers, Colonial Series, America and the West Indies 30, Aug. 1717–Dec. 1718*, edited by Cecil Headlam (London: Cassell & Co., 1930–33), sec. 800, 431.

[8] *Boston News-Letter* no. 776 (Feb. 23–March 2, 1719).

[9] Edward Everett Hale, "Ben Franklin's Ballads," *New England Magazine* 18 (June 1898), 505–7.

A LIVING FROM THE SEA

[1] Hariot, *Briefe and True Report*, 20.

[2] David Stick, *The Outer Banks of North Carolina* (Chapel Hill: University of North Carolina Press, 1958), 212.

[3] Orville Wright to Katharine Wright, Oct. 14, 1900, Family Papers: Correspondence—Wright, Orville, 1900–1902, Wilbur and Orville Wright Papers, Manuscript Division, Library of Congress, Washington, D.C.

[4] Hariot, *Briefe and True Report*, 20.

[5] John Brickell, *The Natural History of North-Carolina* (Dublin, Ireland: James Carson, 1737), 215.

[6] Orlandah Phillips, interview by Bruce Weber, Feb. 18, 1980, interview #010, CALO Oral History Project, Cape Lookout National Seashore.

[7] Sarah Downing, "State record blue marlin still stands," *Outer Banks Sentinel*, June 2, 2007.

[8] Susan Van Dongen, "Hanging Out On The Outer Banks In A Rustic Fishing Camp On An All-but-deserted Barrier Island, Luxuries Are Few: How Romantic Could This Be?" Permission granted by Susan Van Dongen, freelance travel correspondent. Article originally published in *Philadelphia Inquirer* Travel Section, July 21, 1996.

[9] Beth Finke, "A Fish Story." Permission granted by National Federation of the Blind—www.nfb.org, June 13, #3, summer edition,

July 22, 1998, *Voice of the Diabetic*.

[10] Morgan Jones, "Local Catch, the Reel World: Kids Ask a Fisherman About His Career," *Coastwatch* (Summer 2013). Reprinted with permission from *Coastwatch*, a magazine from North Carolina Sea Grant, ncseagrant.org.

HURRICANES

[1] Douglas Stover, *U.S. Weather Bureau Station, Hatteras, North Carolina*, *Special Historic Resource Study* (National Park Service, 2007), 16.

[2] Ibid., 1.

[3] "Racer's Storm, October 1837," North Carolina Shipwrecks, March 30, 2012, http://northcarolinashipwrecks.blogspot.com/2012/03/racers-storm-september-1837.html. Accessed Dec. 2, 2014.

[4] http://northcarolinashipwrecks.blogspot.com/2012/03/hurricanes-of-july-15-august-24-1842.html. Accessed Dec. 2, 2014.

[5] Charles Harry Whedbee, "How Oregon Inlet Got Its Name," *Outer Banks Tales to Remember* (Winston-Salem, N.C.: John F. Blair, Publisher, 1985), 16–22.

[6] Stover, *U.S. Weather Bureau Station*, 15–17.

[7] Gordon Willis, interview by Jan Willis Gillikin, March 29, 1987, Cape Lookout Oral History Project.

[8] Linda E. Nunn, "Islanders remember Emily's devastation," *Island Free Press*, Aug. 2, 2013. Permission granted by *Island Free Press* (www.islandfreepress.org).

[9] "Western Carolina University Students Help Analyze Irene's Damage on NC Outer Banks," http://www.wcu.edu/WebFiles/PDFs/Dredging_Today_Sep_11.pdf. Accessed Dec. 2, 2014.

"FERAL PONY-SIZED HORSES"

[1] Corolla Wild Horse Fund, "2015 Fact Sheet."

[2] "CWHF Horse Sponsorship Overview," Corolla Wild Horse Fund Incorporated, http://www.corollawildhorses.com/sponsorship_overview/, 2012. Accessed Feb. 10, 2015.

[3] Fred Hurteau, "Finding the Wild Horses of Corolla: A Little 4WD Adventure," CarolinaOuterBanks.com. Permission granted by Fred Hurteau, CarolinaOuterBanks.com.

[4] Carl Goerch, *Ocracoke* (Winston-Salem, N.C.: John F. Blair, Publisher, 1956), 101–4.

[5] Bob Brooks, "Riders of the Beach," *Boys' Life* (March 1956), 24, 69.

[6] Carolyn Salter Mason, interview by Connie Mason, Dec. 17, 2010, interview CALO 10-007, Cape Lookout National Seashore.

[7] BJ Mountford, "The 1999 Roundup," written for this volume, Jan. 2015.

THE CIVIL WAR

[1] David D. Porter, *The Naval History of the Civil War* (New York: Sherman Publishing Co., 1886), 44–47.

[2] Claiborne Snead, *Address by Col. Claiborne Snead at the Reunion of the Third Georgia Regiment, at Union Point on the 31st July, 1874...* (Chronicle and Sentinel Job Printing Establishment, 1874).

[3] J. H. E. Whitney, *The Hawkins Zouaves: Their Battles and Marches* (New York: 1866), 65.

[4] Henry T. Clark to Judah P. Benjamin, Feb. 1, 1862, The American Civil War, http://www.civilwar-online.com/2012/02/february-1-1862-north-carolina-governor.html. Accessed Nov. 20, 2014.

[5] Augustus Woodbury and Ambrose Everts Burnside, *Major General A. E. Burnside and the Ninth Army Corps* (Providence, R.I.: Sidney S. Rider & Brother, 1867), 32–33.

[6] D. L. Day, *My Diary of Rambles with the 25th Mass. Volunteer Infantry* (Milford, Mass: King & Billings, 1884), 23–24, 37–38.

[7] Horace James to the Public, June 27, 1863, Letters Received, Department of North Carolina, Record Group 393, part 1, series 3238, Box 2, National Archives.

[8] "Roanoke Island: Letter from Mrs. Freeman," *Freedmen's Advocate* 1 (Aug. 1864), 25–26.

[9] Joseph Tillett et al. to the Assistant Commissioner, Bureau of Refugees, Freedmen, and Abandoned Lands, Dec. 4, 1866, Letters and Orders Received, Reports, and Supply Requests, Roanoke Island, Records of the Assistant Commissioner for North Carolina, Record Group 105, Series 2821, National Archives.

THE LIGHTHOUSES

[1] *United States Light-House Establishment, Instructions to Light-Keepers, July, 1881* (Washington: GPO, 1881), 4, 5, 6, 29.

[2] Orlandah Phillips, interview by Bruce Weber, Feb. 18, 1980, interview #010, Cape Lookout Oral History Project.

[3] "Sinks Lightship off Cape Hatteras," *New York Times*, Aug. 8, 1918.

[4] Jenny Edwards, *To Illuminate the Dark Space: Oral Histories of the Currituck Beach Lighthouse*, edited by Beth P. Storie (Outer Banks Conservationists), 52. Courtesy of Outer Banks Conservationists, Inc.

[5] Ben Dixon MacNeill, *The Hatterasman* (Reprint, Wilmington: Publishing Laboratory of UNC Wilmington, 2008), 191–94.

[6] Rany Jennett, "Cape Hatteras Lighthouse As I Knew It," National Park Service, Cape Hatteras National Seashore.

[7] "Let Lighthouse Go," *Daily Press* (Newport News, Va.), Dec. 20, 1989.

THE LIFESAVING STATIONS

[1] Clarence P. Brady, USCG (Ret.), Letter to the editor, *Coast Guard Magazine* (March 1954), 2.

[2] "Loungings in the Footsteps of the Pioneers," *Harper's New Monthly Magazine* 20 (May 1860).

[3] "A Terrible Loss of Life," *New York Times*, Feb. 1, 1878.

[4] Douglas Stover, *Pea Island Life-Saving Station Historic Resource Study* (National Park Service, 2008), 22–33.

[5] *Annual Report of the Operations of the United States Life-Saving Service for the fiscal year ending June 30, 1894* (Washington: GPO, 1895), 211.

[6] John Allen Midgett Jr. (keeper), logbook entry at Chicamacomico Life-Saving Station, N.C., Aug. 16, 1918.

THE HUNT CLUBS

[1] William K. Boyd, ed., *William Byrd's Histories of the Dividing Line Betwixt Virginia and North Carolina* (Raleigh: North Carolina Historical Commission, 1929), 55.

[2] John Bronson, "In Currituck and Dare," *Forest & Stream* 17 (Apr. 28, 1881), 245.

[3] "The Kitty Hawk Bay Club," *Forest & Stream* (Apr. 28, 1881), 243.

[4] Bronson, 244–45.

[5] Hortense Poyner Parkerson, *Swan Island, Flyway Stopover* (H. P. Parkerson, 1988). Permission granted by Terry M. Parkerson.

[6] Travis Morris, *Duck Hunting on Currituck Sound: Tales from a Native Gunner* (Charleston, S.C.: History Press, 2006). Reprinted by permission of The History Press.

[7] Melinda Lukei, "History of Mackay Island," Knotts Island Scrapbook, http://kiscrapbook.knottsislandonline.com/mackeyisland.html. Reprinted with permission from Melinda Jones Lukei.

[8] Frederick C. Havemeyer, "Currituck Sound," in *Duck Shooting Along the Atlantic Tidewater*, 2nd ed., edited by Eugene V. Connett (New York: William Morrow, 1947), 196–200.

[9] *Margaret M. West et al., Petitioners, v. Earl F. Slick et al., Respondents*, no. 111PA83, 326 S.E. 2d 601 (1985), Supreme Court of North Carolina.

THE BROTHERS FROM OHIO

[1] Orville Wright to Major Lester D. Gardner, Aug. 28, 1945, in Marvin W. McFarland, ed., *Papers of Wilbur and Orville Wright*, vol. 2 (New York: McGraw-Hill, 1953), 1176.

[2] Wilbur Wright to the Smithsonian Institution, May 30, 1899, General Correspondence: Smithsonian Institution, 1889–1909, Wilbur and Orville Wright Papers, Manuscript Division, Library of Congress, Washington, D.C.

[3] William Tate to Wilbur Wright, Aug. 18, 1900, General Correspondence: Tate, William J., 1900–1909, Wilbur and Orville Wright Papers, Manuscript Division, Library of Congress, Washington, D.C.

[4] Wilbur Wright to Katharine Wright, Oct. 18, 1903, Family Papers: Correspondence—Wright, Wilbur, 1903–1905, Wilbur and Orville Wright Papers, Manuscript Division, Library of Congress, Washington, D.C.

[5] Orville Wright's Diary D, Dec. 17, 1903, Manuscripts/Mixed Materials: 1903, Wilbur and Orville Wright Papers, Manuscript Division, Library of Congress, Washington, D.C.

[6] Orville Wright to Bishop Milton Wright (telegram), Dec. 17, 1903,

Family Papers: Correspondence—Wright, Orville, 1903, Wilbur and Orville Wright Papers, Manuscript Division, Library of Congress, Washington, D.C.

[7] "Flying Machine Soars Three Miles in Teeth of High Wind Over Sand Hills and Waves On Carolina Coast," *Norfolk Virginian-Pilot*, Dec. 18, 1903.

[8] David Stick, "Musings of a Maverick," 2002. Paper available through The Outer Banks History Center, Manteo, N.C.

[9] "Address by J. H. Doolittle," *Golden Anniversary Observance of Man's First Successful Powered Flight* (Washington: GPO, 1954), 20.

THE NATIONAL SEASHORES

[1] Robert A. Vogel, address during ceremonial transfer of Cape Lookout Lighthouse from the U.S. Coast Guard to the National Park Service, June 14, 2003.

[2] Joel Hancock, interview by Connie Mason, Feb. 18, 2011, interview CALO 10-020, Cape Lookout National Seashore.

[3] Tony Seamon Jr., interview by Connie Mason, May 28, 2010, interview CALO 10-004, Cape Lookout National Seashore.

[4] Frank Stick, "A Coastal Park for North Carolina and the Nation," *Elizabeth City Independent*, July 21, 1933.

[5] Cameron Binkley, *The Creation and Establishment of Cape Hatteras National Seashore* (Atlanta: Cultural Resources Division, National Park Service, 2007), 215–16.

[6] Matthew Godfrey, "The World According to Me," seaturtle.org, www.seaturtle.org/blog/mgodfrey/2004_08.shtml. Permission granted by Matthew Godfrey.

[7] Walter B. Jones, "Where I Stand," Congressman Walter Jones, http://jones.house.gov/issue/energy-environment-lands. Accessed Aug. 22, 2014.

[8] "House Again Passes Jones' Bill," Outer Banks Preservation Association, http://www.obpa.org/, Feb. 6, 2014. Accessed Aug. 22, 2014.

[9] Ted Williams, "Outer Banks of North Carolina Become a Bloody Beachhead," Forbes.com, http://www.forbes.com/sites/deborahljacobs/2012/09/04/outer-banks-of-north-carolina-become-a-bloody-beachhead/, Sept. 4, 2012. Accessed Sept. 17, 2013. Permission granted by Ted Williams.

WORLD WAR II

[1] Nell Wise Wechter, *Taffy of Torpedo Junction* (Reprint, Chapel Hill: University of North Carolina Press, 1996), 64–66. Copyright © 1996 by Marcia Wechter Kass. Foreword © 1996 by the University of North Carolina Press. Used by permission of the publisher, www.uncpress.unc.edu.

[2] "MS *City of New York*," http://home.comcast.net/~cshortridge/ MERSHIPHIS/AMERISHIPL/MS_CITY_OF_NEW _YORK.pdf. Accessed Aug. 24, 2014. Permission granted by Clayton C. Shortridge.

[3] L. Van Loan Naisawald, *In Some Foreign Field: The Story of Four British Graves on the Outer Banks* (Winston-Salem, N.C.: John F. Blair, Publisher, 1972), 33, 38–39. Permission granted by Publications Branch, Historical Research Office, Office of Archives & History, N.C. Department of Cultural Resources.

[4] "Two in Civil Air Patrol Lose Lives off New Inlet," *Daily Advance*, Dec. 26, 1942. Reprinted with permission from *Daily Advance*, Elizabeth City, N.C.

[5] Naisawald, *In Some Foreign Field*, 79-80.

[6] Gordon Willis, interview by Jan Willis Gillikin, March 29, 1987, Cape Lookout Oral History Project.

[7] Jakie Robertson, interview by Connie Mason, July 31, 1985, interview 62, Cape Lookout Oral History Project.

[8] O. Lawrence Burnette Jr., *Son of Carolina: A Memoir* (Baltimore, Md.: Publish America, 2011). Permission granted by American Star Books.

[9] Reinhard Hardegen, interview by Stephen Ames, 1992, "The Commander Interviews," uboat.net, www.uboat.net/men/interviews/ hardegen.htm. Accessed Nov. 9, 2014.

THE TOURIST TRADE

[1] "Nag's Head Hotel," *Elizabeth City Sentinel*, in *Semi-Weekly Standard* (Raleigh, N.C.), Sept. 23, 1857.

[2] "Nags Head Hotel Reddens the Heavens with Its Ruin," *North Carolinian* (Raleigh, N.C.), July 30, 1903.

[3] Susan Byrum Rountree, *Nags Headers* (Winston-Salem, N.C.: John F. Blair, Publisher, 2001), 22, 24, 26. Permission granted by Susan Byrum Rountree.

[4] Rountree, 71–72.

[5] Paul Green, *The Lost Colony: A Symphonic Drama of American History* (Chapel Hill and London: University of North Carolina Press, 2001), 123–25. Copyright © 2001 by The Paul Green Foundation and Laurence G. Avery. Used by permission of the University of North Carolina Press. www.uncpress.unc.edu.

[6] Ibid., 104–5.

[7] Livestream, http://new.livestream.com/accounts/191743/ CarlKasell, Apr. 16, 2013. Accessed Nov. 18, 2014. Courtesy of the University of North Carolina at Chapel Hill Library.

[8] Ray McAllister, *Ocracoke: The Pearl of the Outer Banks* (Rocky Mount, N.C.: Beach Glass Books), 162. Courtesy of Ray McAllister.

[9] Circanceast.beaufortccc.edu/BCCC/articles/Spring1984/PDF/ Story3.pdf. Accessed Sept. 24, 2014. Courtesy of Beaufort County Community College.

[10] David B. Eisendrath (1914-1988), "A Tribute to Aycock," *Aycock Brown's Outer Banks*, edited by David Stick (Norfolk, Va.: Donning Co., 1976), 13.

[11] Aycock Brown, "Oregon Inlet Bass Fishing Best Since 1947, Say Observers," *Gaston Gazette*, May 7, 1949. Courtesy of *Gaston Gazette*.

[12] "Aycock Brown: Covering the Waterfront," *Gaston Gazette*, Dec. 10, 1949. Courtesy of *Gaston Gazette*.

[13] "Aycock Brown: Covering the Waterfront," *Gaston Gazette*, July 29, 1950. Courtesy of *Gaston Gazette*.

[14] Aycock Brown, "Story of Hatteras' Biggest Shark Is Repeated As Legend," *Daily Times-News* (Burlington, N.C.), Nov. 17, 1952 .

BY SEA, LAND, AND AIR

[1] Goerch, 25–35.

[2] Barbara Brannon, *The Ferries of North Carolina: Traveling the State's Nautical Highways* (Wilmington, N.C.: Winoca Press, 2007), 18–19. Used by permission of Winoca Press.

[3] Anderson Midgett, taped interview by Beth Midgett, "Midgett Family Comments," Outer Banks Task Force, July 2, 2010.

[4] Theodore Stockton Midgett Jr., taped interview by Beth Midgett, "Midgett Family Comments," Outer Banks Task Force, July 2, 2010.

[5] Rebuilding N.C. 12, http://nc12repairs.blogspot.com/. Accessed Nov. 10, 2014.

[6] Glenn McVicker, "Bonner Bridge: Driving on Water," *Our State* (Jan. 2012). Reprinted with permission of *Our State*.

[7] Chris Houston, adapted from his blogpost, "In Blackbeard's Wake," http://warrior481.blogspot.com/2013/08/in-wake-of-blackbeard.html, Aug. 31, 2013. Permission granted by Chris Houston.

General Reading

Barefoot, Daniel W. *Touring the Backroads of North Carolina's Lower Coast*. Winston-Salem, N.C.: John F. Blair, Publisher, 1995.

————. *Touring the Backroads of North Carolina's Upper Coast*. Winston-Salem, N.C.: John F. Blair, Publisher, 1995.

Barnes, Jay. *North Carolina's Hurricane History*, 3rd ed. Chapel Hill: University of North Carolina Press, 2001.

Brannon, Barbara. *The Ferries of North Carolina: Traveling the State's Nautical Highways*. Wilmington, N.C.: Winoca Press, 2007.

Connett, Eugene V., ed. *Duck Shooting Along the Atlantic Tidewater*, 2nd ed. New York: William Morrow, 1947.

Crouch, Tom. *The Bishop's Boys: A Life of Wilbur and Orville Wright*. New York: W. W. Norton, 1989.

Duffus, Kevin P. *War Zone: World War II off the North Carolina Coast*. Raleigh, N.C.: Looking Glass Productions, 2012.

Gannon, Michael. *Operation Drumbeat: The Dramatic True Story of Germany's First U-Boat Attacks Along the American Coast in World War II*. New York: HarperCollins, 1990.

Goerch, Carl. *Ocracoke*. Winston-Salem, N.C.: John F. Blair, Pulisher, 1956.

Green, Paul. *The Lost Colony: A Symphonic Drama of American History*. Chapel Hill and London: University of North Carolina Press, 2001.

Johnson, Captain Charles. *A General History of the Pyrates...*, 2nd ed. London: T. Warner, 1724.

Johnson, Clint. *Touring the Carolinas' Civil War Sites*, 2nd ed. Winston-Salem, N.C.: John F. Blair, Publisher, 2011.

Kirk, Stephen. *First in Flight: The Wright Brothers in North Carolina*. Winston-Salem, N.C.: John F. Blair, Publisher, 1995.

Lee, Robert E. *Blackbeard the Pirate: A Reappraisal of His Life and Times*. Winston-Salem, N.C.: John F. Blair, Publisher, 1974.

Lloyd, Jared. "The Story of the Rise and Fall of the Currituck Hunt Clubs," NCBeaches.com, https://www.ncbeaches.com/Features/Wildlife/HistoryofCurrituckHuntClubs/, 2006–7. Accessed July 30, 2014.

MacNeill, Ben Dixon. *The Hatterasman*. Wilmington, N.C.: Publishing Laboratory of UNC Wilmington, 2008.

McAllister, Ray. *Hatteras Island: Keeper of the Outer Banks*. Winston-Salem, N.C.: John F. Blair, Publisher, 2009.

———. *Ocracoke: The Pearl of the Outer Banks*. Rocky Mount, N.C.: Beach Glass Books, 2013.

McNaughton, Marimar. *Outer Banks Architecture: An Anthology of Outposts, Lodges, and Cottages*. Winston-Salem, N.C.: John F. Blair, Publisher, 2000.

Mobley, Joe A. *Ship Ashore! The U.S. Lifesavers of Coastal North Carolina*. Raleigh: Office of Archives and History, N.C. Department of Cultural Resources, 1994.

Naisawald, L. Van Loan. *In Some Foreign Field: The Story of Four British Graves on the Outer Banks*. Winston-Salem, N.C.: John F. Blair, Publisher, 1972.

Prioli, Carmine. *The Wild Horses of Shackleford Banks*. Winston-Salem, N.C.: John F. Blair, Publisher, 2007.

Rights, Douglas L. *The American Indian in North Carolina*, 2nd ed. Winston-Salem, N.C.: John F. Blair, Publisher, 1957.

Rountree, Susan Byrum. *Nags Headers*. Winston-Salem, N.C.: John F. Blair, Publisher, 2001.

Schoenbaum, Thomas J. *Islands, Capes, and Sounds: The North Carolina Coast*. Winston-Salem, N.C.: John F. Blair, Publisher, 1982.

Stick, David. *Graveyard of the Atlantic: Shipwrecks of the North Carolina Coast*. Chapel Hill: University of North Carolina Press, 1952.

———. *North Carolina Lighthouses*. Raleigh: Division of Archives and History, N.C. Department of Cultural Resources, 1980.

———. *The Outer Banks of North Carolina*. Chapel Hill: University of North Carolina Press, 1958.

Stick, David, ed. *Aycock Brown's Outer Banks*. Norfolk, Va.: Donning, 1976.

———. *An Outer Banks Reader*. Chapel Hill and London: University of North Carolina Press, 1998.

Trotter, William R. *Ironclads and Columbiads: The Civil War in North Carolina, The Coast*. Winston-Salem, N.C.: John F. Blair, Publisher, 1989.

Index